Light & Fire

NANCY PFAFF

Light & Fire

A SPIRITUAL BIOGRAPHY OF
DANNY E. MORRIS

Providence House Publishers
PROVIDENCE PUBLISHING CORPORATION
FRANKLIN, TENNESSEE

Printed in the United States of America

06   05   04   03   02   1   2   3   4   5

Library of Congress Catalog Card Number: 2002105564

ISBN: 1-57736-263-2

Cover illustration by Nancy Pfaff

Cover design by Gary Bozeman

Structural editing by Charla Honea, WordWeavers

Verse translation from *The Psalms: A New Translation for Prayer and Worship*, by Gary Chamberlain.

Providence House Publishers

PROVIDENCE PUBLISHING CORPORATION

238 Seaboard Lane • Franklin, Tennessee 37067
800-321-5692
www.providencepubcorp.com

Remember those who led you,
who spoke the word of God to you;
and considering the result of their conduct,
imitate their faith.
Jesus Christ is the same yesterday and today,
yes and forever.
—Hebrews 13:7–8 NASB

Contents

Feb 2003

Foreword

If you have not read his books, you have probably heard a preacher or teacher speak of Brother Lawrence. Like many others, Brother Lawrence entered a monastic order believing he was giving up this world's happiness to become a monk. Instead, he discovered a much deeper happiness than he'd ever imagined. Reflecting on this turn of events, Brother Lawrence once said to God in prayer, "You have outwitted me."

Danny Morris is one of God's unique creatures. As much as anyone else, he fits the claim that each one of us is an unrepeatable miracle of God. It has been my good pleasure to walk with Danny and to have his friendship, an intimate friendship, for a huge hunk of our lives.

I met him first when we were students at Candler School of Theology, Emory University in Atlanta. My hunch is that only someone with special gifts of seeing into the future would have ever thought that Danny Morris would make the impact on persons and on the church that he has made. There was a sense among all of our classmates that Danny might have been the most unlikely one to succeed. It wasn't that he wasn't bright or gifted—it was his humor. He just never seemed to take anything seriously enough to make a difference. It didn't matter the occasion or the conversation, he always made us laugh.

God outwitted us. God enabled Danny to turn his capacity for humor into a great spiritual gift, ministering to people and providing avenues of healing through laughter. Danny came to know with Norman Cousins that giggling is always more healthy than gargling.

He surprised us all with the woman he married. None of us could believe that Rosalie would have given him a second look, much less a second thought. They seemed so completely different—but what a couple they have been, each complementing the other and building a life of discipleship and a unique life of prayer together.

Danny and I parted ways after seminary. He went to Florida; I went to Mississippi. The civil rights upheaval in Mississippi in the early 1960s eventuated in my going to California—so we really were out of touch for fifteen years. Then God outwitted us both.

In the midst of my ministry in California, I learned about the John Wesley Great Experiment or Ten Brave Christians. To my surprise, this had begun in Danny's church. That movement—which his biographer describes in this book—impacted the church tremendously. I was on a similar pilgrimage myself—small groups, prayer, and earnest discipline in an effort to demonstrate Christian discipleship. As a result of that John Wesley Great Experiment, Danny was invited to the staff of the Board of Discipleship. Not long after that, I was invited to lead a prayer movement for the Upper Room. Thus began ten of the most significant years of my life and the life of my family.

We moved into the same neighborhood with Danny and Rosalie in Mt. Juliet, Tennessee. The two families became inseparable and our children grew up together. We owned a secondhand lawn mower together. Though we knew little or nothing about horses, we bought horses. We helped each other build a barn for our horses. For ten years Danny and I were together every week and almost every week our families were together. What memorable, hilarious times. My wife, Jerry, remembers how much we laughed. She observed, "God must have a sense of humor. Often we didn't know when we had moved from laughter to prayer."

Danny and I commuted together to our jobs in Nashville—always a thirty-five- or forty-minute drive. It was on those drives that we shared our lives—the deepest corners of our lives, ministering to each other, encouraging each other, holding each other accountable. Everything we wrote during those years, we read to each other as we drove back and forth. *The Workbook of Living*

Prayer, my most significant contribution to the church, was born and came to completion on those rides back and forth. The Adventure in Living Prayer, the "Prayer In My Life" series, the Living Prayer Center, the "I Care" program, "Resurgence '76," The Upper Room Prayer Packet, the seed thoughts for the magazine *Weavings,* the beginning framework of the Academy for Spiritual Formation, the Emmaus movement—all were a part of our life together.

I had been invited to join the staff of the Upper Room to direct a ministry, primarily calling people to a life of prayer, providing direction and resources for growth in and practice of prayer, and giving structure through the *Upper Room Magazine* to a united call to prayer by people around the world. During those days, I knew no one within the Protestant tradition was talking about *spiritual formation*. The Roman Catholics have known the importance of this aspect of Christian growth and have used "formation" language through the centuries. On our way to work one day we agreed that "spiritual formation" was a rich concept similar to the Wesleyan principles of growing in grace and maturing in Christ, and that we could introduce the term to the denomination through the Upper Room. Just as we were driving under the Donelson Pike overpass, we shook hands in agreement. This is how we worked together across ten wonderful years. It wasn't long before we at the Upper Room were talking about spiritual formation and seeking to provide resources for a broader expression of spirituality than we had known before.

About three years after I became a part of the Upper Room, working in the area of prayer and spiritual formation, I was invited to become the world editor of the *Upper Room*. Danny was on the staff of the Board of Evangelism. I invited him to take my place, and after a long season of discernment he responded and thus all the things that came out of those years of our ministry together evolved.

I doubt if there's been another person that I've shared more deeply with over such a long period of time as I shared with Danny. So, I'm happy that Nancy Pfaff has written this book. No one could ever capture all that Danny and Rosalie Morris are, but here is enough of a testimony to give you a flavor of a life well lived.

Danny and Rosalie are two of God's marvelous witnesses. No one who has known them could doubt their confidence in God's grace and God's power. No one who has known them has not been lifted by their love and encouragement. No one who has been with them for even a short time has not been able to move from taking life too seriously to laughing and lightening up in their approach to life, thus finding a new kind of energy. No one who has known them has not been inspired to be more themselves and in being more themselves, give more of themselves in commitment to the Lord. Reading this book will give you an idea of the expansiveness, the depth, and the commitment of these lives.

It was toward the end of his active ministry that Danny began his work in the area of discernment. This work has not received the attention it deserves and may be his most notable contribution to the whole church. It is no wonder that he pursued a study of and has shared about discernment. He has sought to live so close to the Lord and in the center of the Lord's will that he knows the importance of it. But even with all he knows about discernment— my hunch is he would say with me, "God always outwits us."

Maxie D. Dunnam
President, Asbury Theological Seminary

Preface & Acknowledgments

Danny E. Morris is a simple, ordinary man who, by virtue of his faith walk, is able to have impact on others through a living relationship with the Divine and by bringing renewal to the church.

Whether you read this simply for encouragement or to study, you may see more clearly how your own spiritual and ministerial journey has progressed and how you may profit from some things Danny has learned.

Danny E. Morris, a country boy from the South, discovered the power of laypersons when some members of a church he served committed to put God first. After twenty-two years in the local church pastorate, he was called to Nashville, to one of the major church boards of United Methodism, the General Board of Discipleship. From this platform, he has been able to influence congregations unnumbered and to call people to experience the fire only God can bring.

Not only was Methodism in America and abroad impacted, his influence touched other denominations at home as well. Today his ministry continues to impact Methodism but also crosses denominational boundaries. It is focused in some challenging ways through the ministry of prayer, through the Academy for Spiritual Formation, and the Spiritual Discernment Network.

As you complete the reading of each chapter, consider the prompts in Appendix A. Have a notebook handy if any one of them invites you to go further in consideration of your faith journey. "Ministry" is interpreted here as belonging to lay and clergy, alike. Let's explore how this passion for renewal was

kindled and discover more about the fire that burns in his heart
and imagination.

▨ ▨ ▨

Realizing that mentoring is a key to success in any job or
ministry, I am especially grateful to Dr. James Robert Clinton,
professor of Leadership Training at the School of World Mission
in Pasadena, California. His research of over five hundred
Christian leaders has led to findings that there are identifiable
stages and lessons leaders must negotiate to actualize their leadership potential. His writings have especially empowered me in
authoring this biography.

I certainly have to mention Danny Morris in this litany of
gratitude. We worked together hand-in-glove. No author ever
had any better support in the writing process. He provided the
"color" for the framework I set before him and much more.
What I had envisioned as a thirty-five-page summary of leadership lessons that he learned over a lifetime became the current
volume.

Another key person in the process was Maxie Dunnam,
who provided a candid interview about his friend and
colleague Danny, and contributed the foreword to this book. A
third essential supporter of the project was Sam Teague, who
told me about Danny and identified financial sources necessary
to the book's completion. Both read the manuscript and made
valuable suggestions.

Without the financial contributions of Brave Christian
Associates, Inc., this book might still be searching for resources
to make it possible. They have been generous beyond anything I
could imagine.

Many contributed through interviews and written material,
among them the Morris family—Rosalie, Alan, David, and
Diana; Happy Woodman, Faye L. Davis, Merle B. Jackson, Mary
Stamps, Reverend Claude Whitehead, Elise Eslinger, and Stephen
Bryant. There are many others not named here who gave sugges-
tions and read the manuscript.

To all these, I am indebted and deeply grateful.

CHAPTER ONE

The Preparation of Childhood

"And there was light . . . "—Gen. 1:3

Just Enough for Seeing

God's sovereign work, especially one's calling, is very crucial in the development of a leader. Danny E. Morris's life exemplifies this work. It is vital that we recognize and embrace our childhood and adolescent experiences, because they lay the foundation for our future ministry effectiveness or failure. Our response to the events of this stage can propel us forward or cripple us. As we look at this stage in Danny's life, you may wish to keep a pad and pencil nearby as your own memories surface. This way you can be encouraged where your strengths are revealed and see where your weaknesses are rooted and how you are progressing.

Danny was born November 14, 1933, on what was known as the Bullard Farm about three or four miles outside of Glendale, Florida. He was the second son of Lucy and Dan Morris and brother of Robert de Leon—Bobby—five years older. It was not an easy birth, and his mother hemorrhaged badly. The family doctor came out from town to stay with them overnight. God would use this doctor sixteen years later to teach Danny what would become the core of his philosophy of ministry.

The year 1933 was right at the end of the depression. The Morris family were farmers in a depleted area. They had very little income from any source. Danny's mother could not write her mother often because there was no money for a three-cent stamp. When Dan asked what it would take to settle up with the doctor who delivered the new baby, he said he would take twelve gallons of cane syrup. This took two to three years to pay off. Danny jokingly says that is why he has always been a sweet child.

1

Danny's mother was a preacher's kid. Her father was "Old Brother Sellers," lovingly referred to as "a saintly man." Danny heard all his life about him, "Oh son, I knew your grandpa. There was nobody like him. If anybody was a saint, he was."

Old Brother Sellers picked his grandson Danny, the only one of twenty-seven grandchildren, to dedicate to God for the ministry, "to follow in his footsteps." He took Danny as an infant into his bedroom by himself and carefully knelt down beside the bed. Holding Danny on the bed with his hands under him, he prayed and dedicated him to God for service in the ministry. He did this numerous times. This is a key to Danny's sense of *why* and *how* so much has happened in his life. Providence, through Danny's mother, would save this story for him until he decided whether or not he would go into ministry.

Dan and Lucy Morris were very hard-working people. When Danny was just a year old, they moved to Glendale, Florida, and ran a little country grocery store, a village grocery called the Glendale Mercantile Store. They later moved to DeFuniak Springs, a sleepy little town of about forty-five hundred people. The city street ran in front of their house. In DeFuniak, the Morris's never worried about their children playing outdoors in the evening. There were neighborhood gangs in the positive sense, kids who played well together. One of their favorite games was football, which was played in the street. Traffic would come and go, and they would keep playing because it came so seldom.

The Christian faith was strongest in Danny's mother, Lucy. Although his father, Dan, was also a believer, he chose not to talk much about it. Dan had grown up a Baptist and became a Methodist when he married Lucy. He attended church with her occasionally. He was a kind of preferred relative among all the relatives who called him Uncle Dan. Dan and Lucy were very close. They ran the business together—shared ideas, values, and esteem for one another. Their love was obvious, though not expressed outwardly. It was deep, very deep, and wonderful.

Danny grew up content and strengthened by the relationship his parents had with each other. It gave him an inner peace, and he had a strong sense of pride that his parents were together and that there never had been a divorce in his family. He knew it happened in other families, but he felt it was so good it never happened to them.

Church meant a lot to Lucy, as did prayer. Her children began to realize how important prayer was when they were old enough to play outside in the summer after breakfast or go to school. Danny has vivid memories of her calling the boys to her, joining hands in a circle, and his mother praying over them for the day. Then she would kiss them and let them go. It was quick, done every day. One day Bobby asked, "Mother, does the Lord always want us to kiss when we pray?" This symbolizes the kind of faith tradition in which Bobby and Danny grew up.

The first glimmer of leadership possibilities occurred in Danny's Methodist Youth Fellowship group where he was president for three or four years. The youth group blossomed with his leadership and also because there were other wonderful youth leaders working with him. This experience had a lot to do with his choosing to go into the ministry. It was a growing, pleasant experience.

During his junior year in high school, Danny was a Future Farmers of America (FFA) student. He was the secretary of their FFA chapter. That year they hit upon the idea to take a group of about twenty on a school bus from Florida to New York City via Washington, D.C. Danny was a prime mover, and as secretary, wrote ahead to FFA chapters in various places asking them to host his group overnight.

Along the way home, the bus was involved in a wreck. No one was hurt, but the bus required three days for repairs. For the following day, arrangements had been made for them to stay overnight in the building of an FFA chapter in a certain town. Danny had exchanged letters with their chapter president. In the fright and confusion caused by the wreck, he forgot all about the contacts he had made. He knew about the sleeping arrangements, but the matter never crossed his mind.

What he didn't know, until he received a letter from them, was that the host FFA chapter had gone all out to plan a big welcome and celebration. They were waiting for Danny's group to arrive—the mayor and the principal were there, and a big supper was prepared. But, without sending the host chapter any indication, Danny's group never showed up. Danny still winces when he remembers that error on his part, and he still feels sad that he dropped the ball.

It was a powerful jolt to what had been his carefree leadership. That haunting memory continues to remind him that being responsible means keeping your eye on the ball at all times. Being responsible is a big word for him.

The summer following his junior year in high school was a season of accelerated change and growth. From the time he was eleven years old, he'd lived with a "snaggle tooth" look, the result of a diving accident. When somebody pushed him off of the diving board, he hit someone's head and broke his front tooth. Because he was eleven, the dentist chose not to provide a denture for another five years. In the summer before his senior year, he got a partial dental plate that removed his snaggle tooth appearance.

During those years he had often felt the hurt of looking different than the other kids. As a defense he used his hand to cover his mouth and humor to try to cover his hurt. His developing sense of humor would become one of his most useful tools in relating to people and handling the challenges of ministry.

When the church youth camp at Huntington College in Montgomery, Alabama, came along, Danny had just received his denture and was feeling on top of the world. He met Mary V. O'Brien who was an excellent pianist. She was an attractive girl with a lot of personality. She and Danny hit it off. Together they became the hit of the camp talent show. Danny was the emcee, and Mary V. provided the music. She had great piano skills, and Danny had wit. Here was more than a hint that performing in public was to be a part of his life in the future.

The day before camp concluded, Danny felt a call to prayer late that afternoon by himself. That night he went forward at the end of an invitation service, then he went back to the dorm. He remembers asking two people, Sy Mathison and Ed Nichols, both preachers in the conference, to come and talk to him. That night he said he wanted to give his life to Christ and enter the ministry.

When Danny went home the next day, he told his parents and his pastor. They were very positive, delighted, and excited. By the time school started in September, it was no secret to anybody in a little town like DeFuniak Springs that Danny was going to be a preacher. With the success of the summer at camp, the flush of a renewed Christian commitment, his restored smile, his upcoming senior year when he hoped to be playing varsity football, Danny felt that September opened with endless possibilities.

A heavy cloud appeared in his skies only weeks later, in late September. His father became ill. Over a two-week period, Danny often went in and sat by his dad's bed praying, yet his dad grew worse and worse. He prayed, "God, don't let my dad die. Please don't let him die. I've given you my life. Give me my father's life."

Danny came home from the hospital one night with Bobby. They left his mother and other relatives at the hospital where family members had gathered from everywhere. Because of so much company the house looked like a fall-out shelter. Danny went out to the backyard. It was a time of feeling desperate and so alone.

It was in late September in North Florida. Danny had on a short sleeve shirt, and stepped out into a cool, brisk night. His dark mood was painfully heavy; he could not see anything in the thick darkness. He felt closed in and choked. It was so dark and awful out there for him by himself. He couldn't hear anything nearby. It was like a deathly silence. The only thing he could hear was a dog barking way off in the distance and an eighteen-wheeler a long ways away going up Vinegar Hill. In the darkness of the night he thought, "I don't hear anything. I don't see anything. I'm totally alone."

Danny walked over to the side of the yard. It was pitch dark, and he could not see. He stopped because he ran into the bushes and realized where he was. He just stood there with his hands in his pockets since it was a little cool. Standing there, stiff as a board like a zombie, racked with impending grief, sixteen years old, he began to try to pray.

This prayer was different than the bargaining prayers he had been praying by his father's bed. This was the hardest prayer he ever prayed then or since. "God, I prayed that my dad would get well, and he grew worse each day. Now I pray that *your will be done*." It took him a long time to get that out, because he had never wanted to pray that before. Rather than God's will, he wanted his own will to be done.

When he prayed it, almost instantly a great sense of peace came over him, a truly wonderful sense of peace. He felt the breeze on his arms, and instead of it making him cold, it felt good and refreshing. He looked up and saw the stars, wondering where they had been. Now they were shining profusely. He heard crickets everywhere, and he was not alone any more.

He noticed his somber mood changed so dramatically that he thought of something totally unrelated that caused him to want to chuckle. His chuckle was an ironic counterpoint to his grief. He was no longer rigid but standing relaxed. He had a peaceful sense that his dad was going to be okay. He went in and found a place to sleep, bedded down, and slept soundly as if nothing had happened.

Bobby awakened him about four hours later to say that their dad had died. Suddenly God and Danny weren't having it so good anymore. He felt he had been tricked in the yard that night. Danny did not pray for a long time. He wondered, "Where was God the night my dad died? What happened to me in the yard that night? What about the peace? What about the stars, the crickets? Why did all that happen to me? What is the meaning of prayer anyway, the purpose of it?" For a sixteen-year-old, these were tough times and hard questions.

While burdened by his confusion and grief, he attended a social gathering in town. One of the guests was their family doctor, the man who had delivered Danny. The doctor called Danny into the adjoining room and said, "Son, I want to tell you about your dad's death." Danny said nothing, just stood there. "If your dad had lived beyond the two weeks of his illness, he would never have spoken again. He would never have walked again. He would never have reasoned again." He thanked the doctor.

Finally, in time, Danny prayed again. "God, I prayed for my dad that he would get well, and he grew worse by the day. And I prayed that your will be done, and you sent chirping crickets and twinkling stars and a peace I could not understand. God, I've just discovered there are some things worse than dying, and I want to thank you for the love and mercy you showed my dad."

Danny describes how he feels about those events:

> That was a deep turning point for me, deeper than I could absorb at sixteen years of age. I have lived on it for years now because it told me something about the will of God. It helped me understand that God's will is the greatest thing that can happen to anybody.
>
> I have heard people say, "I'm afraid of the will of God. I don't want to know God's will. After all, God never asks you to do anything that's fun. If I get too close to God, God might ask me to do something I don't want to do—quit my job, become a missionary, sell my boat."
>
> I often say to myself and sometimes to them, "No, God is not out to get you. God's will is the greatest thing that can happen under any circumstances. I've known that since I was sixteen years old."
>
> That fact is now a great cornerstone of my life and ministry—to say to people and to the church, "Discerning God's will is the most important thing the church must do—and any of us *can* do."

He realized that his prayer for his father to live, when his father would have been severely handicapped, was not for his father's good. Accepting God's will for his father, for his family, and for himself, was a tremendous turning point for Danny. Periodically he has been able to look back at that experience and say it was one of the most formative times of his life. It was a life-shaking experience that has not ceased to shape his life. It is like a continuous spiral. The more his life cycles, the deeper the whole scenario gets for him, the deeper the lessons.

How unusual for a sixteen-year-old to have such an early and deep prayer experience that shook him to his core. It demon-strated his integrity and God's grace on his life. He was able, within a very short time to bow his young heart before his Creator, accepting God's will as good.

Danny's senior high school year was an exciting time. He had one of the leads in the senior class play and enjoyed smiling with the best of them. He was also on the football team and made the first squad. At the end of the season, he discovered that he had been chosen to be on the All-Conference Team. He was shocked and complimented. The coach, aiming to keep him humble, said half seriously, half humorously, "Well, none of the other coaches put a guard up for consideration. I put you up. Since they didn't have anybody else, you got it." A surprising honor had been doused with humility.

Through football Danny learned teamwork, self-discipline, the place of training in reaching a goal, submission to authority, and reward for excellence along with a bit of humility. All these lessons would be used in his work as a pastor and later as one who contributed to the denomination's prayer, evangelism, and small-group ministries.

This same year, Danny's senior year, his mother took a trip and invited him along. During the trip, his mother, Lucy, opened up a family secret. Danny's father had been married and divorced before she married him. Danny had a halfsister, Doris, whom he had never met and had never even heard about. For Danny, who had prided himself on his spotless family background, this was a real blow. He thought that his family was different from so many others where divorce had caused such heartache. In actuality, he was just like everyone else. It was a sobering experience. Both his father's death and this family secret were used by God to plough the character of his soul, grounding his feet in earthy soil.

CHAPTER TWO

The Sophomore Preacher
"Be fruitful. . . ."—Gen. 1:28

In 1951, Danny left DeFuniak Springs for Florida State University (FSU) in Tallahassee. He graduated with a degree in teaching English, but he really majored in college life in general. Debate was his favorite "activity," and he became a collegiate judge of debate competition.

During his first days at the university, Danny did some volunteer work with a pastor from Havana, Florida, near Tallahassee. It wasn't that he was so dedicated, but his girlfriend lived there. One day, Dr. Joe A. Tolle, the district superintendent called him and offered Danny a position pastoring the East Leon Circuit. He was a sophomore in college by then and only nineteen when he became a pastor that February. The likability which his teachers, coaches, and peers appreciated about him in high school began to open doors for him in a larger arena.

He was appointed as pastor of three rural churches with a total of 225 members. He was a kid with no experience and no training. He drove between Chaires, Lloyd, and Miccosukee, Florida, tending the Methodist churches there. He worked the circuit for twenty-eight months, until he graduated. It was a tough assignment. Not only was Danny going to college, he was dating full time while covering the churches. Dating often came first.

Later he realized he wasn't so involved in his own personal life that he couldn't experience the distress of those he ministered to. In Chaires (named after the Chaires family), a little town of maybe twenty-five people, the center of town life was the post office. During Danny's stay, the postal service chose to close that

post office. It was like death for the community because the
people would no longer be known to anybody outside Chaires,
only to each other. It was a terrible feeling of loss of identity for
them and Danny entered into it with them. He had never watched
a community die before.

He was making two thousand dollars a year and had a house
to live in. This was big bucks for a student back then. The two
smallest churches paid him five hundred dollars each and the
larger one thousand dollars. He didn't have to do it alone either.
His mother, Lucy, Old Brother Sellers's daughter, came over and
lived with Danny there in the parsonage, acting as the parsonage
hostess. She closed her house during that time and supported
Danny as mother, friend, helper, and prayer partner.

As often happens with firsts, Danny's first church board
meeting was a baptism by fire. They met at the parsonage with
probably ten people present. They had taken care of all the
church business, so they called on Danny to say something as the
new pastor. He felt a need to do a half-time coach's pep talk. This
particular audience was from the smallest country church. They
probably had thirty people on a Sunday morning.

He put on his best, earnest look and with all seriousness said,
"You know there are a lot of people around here who don't come
to church. If you will tell me who I need to go see first, I'll be glad
to go see them, see if we can get them started coming. You know
people, and you have friends. It would be wonderful if you could
contact them and invite them to come to church. It's a new time
for us now, and that's the way we can build up church attendance, make this church really come alive."

An older man named Arthur was there. He was well beyond
retirement age. He was rather outspoken and could be combative.
For many people, he wasn't easy to be around. He interrupted
Danny's motivational talk with, "Preacher, if you want to build up
this church, put a William Jennings Bryan in the pulpit!"

That froze the group, and Danny was shocked and offended.
Without thinking, he replied, "Mr. Ellis can you get William
Jennings Bryan for five hundred dollars a year?" Well, the group
went from quiet to just plain frozen. The new pastor and the
group's "thorn in the flesh" had just sent a volley back and forth.

The Sophomore Preacher

Arthur slapped his leg and said with a twinkle in his eye, "I believe you've got somethin'." And that room exploded in laughter. It was a welcome release of the tremendous pressure, and they laughed and laughed and laughed. Danny laughed and Arthur laughed and they soon ended the meeting. Arthur and Danny never again had a confrontational moment. They lived next door to each other, with Arthur spending uncounted hours coming over and helping Danny totally remodel the parsonage inside and out. Others did help, but Arthur probably put in two hundred to three hundred hours. He was retired and had all kinds of tools. He also knew carpentry and electrical work. They became good friends as a result of that night. The humor God developed in Danny over his adolescence was now bearing its fruit in ministry. This quality would provide a life preserver in the occasional stormy waters of church life over many years.

Danny's concern that others be invited to the church resulted from his innate evangelistic gift, although at that time, he wasn't aware of having that gift. All he really knew was that there were vacant seats that he thought should be filled with people. He wanted to preach to a full house. He knew they needed to work on evangelism, reach people, bring them in, and help the church to come alive. That first ministry motivation continues to be at the heart of his ministry today.

During Danny's twenty-eight months on the circuit, he learned just how patient, loving, kind, longsuffering, and tolerant people could be with a nineteen-year-old trying to balance pastoring and a college education. These people were his best friends. There was a downside as well. Danny had grown up in a strong, vibrant church, and the three churches he pastored were struggling country churches. Instead of people being enthusiastic and ready for new vision, the attitude was one of resignation, "Well, you can't expect much out of us 'cause we are a small church, and we can't do much." The burden of that kind of setting for doing ministry got to be heavy.

This first ministry experience on the East Leon Circuit helped Danny build on his use of humor to ease relationships. It also increased his administrative know-how in handling a busy schedule and developing new ideas for these small churches.

Added to this was his emerging awareness of the value of having a woman in the parsonage who could partner with him in ministry. He got a good look at both the joys and sorrows of being a pastor. When he graduated from Florida State, he went on to the Candler School of Theology at Emory University near Atlanta, Georgia.

At Candler, Danny focused on the Old and New Testaments together with practical ministry courses. Although he didn't have an appointment the first year, he worked with youth for nine months at Sandy Springs Methodist Church in Sandy Springs, Georgia, just north of Atlanta. During this time he met Rosalie, a student nurse. He says that within three weeks after they met "she asked for my hand in marriage." Rosalie let him know early on that she was a Christian before she was a preacher's wife. Any role a church might want her to fulfill would have to first be identified as God's will for her. She has been Danny's partner, wife, lover, and she has always pulled him forward spiritually. With Rosalie's influence, and his increased maturity and responsibility, his grades at seminary went from Bs and Cs to As and Bs during his two final years.

During his second year in seminary, he was appointed to Mt. Gilead, a student appointment, a station church with about seventy-five members but no parsonage. He and Rosalie were married two months later. For the most part, the people were pleasant and appreciative, salt-of-the-earth kind of people. They had never had much in a preacher, so they didn't expect much of Danny.

Rosalie and Danny learned that she was pregnant. They had been married on August 5, 1956, and were blessed by their first child, Alan, on June 16 the following year. They were excited and delighted about the pregnancy. Of course, since Rosalie was pregnant so soon, the first question Danny's mother had was, "When is this baby due?" In those days people were very watchful that first babies came a full nine months or longer after the wedding.

Danny had never thought to inquire about the due date, and when his mother asked, he just guessed, "Oh, sometime next March or April. His mother said, "Son . . . that doesn't give us enough time." She was troubled until Rosalie told her the date. There was plenty of time, with two weeks to spare.

While Rosalie was in the hospital having Alan, Danny met with Dr. Nat Long, the district superintendent, who surprised him with the news, "I've got you a bigger church." Danny wanted to know what he meant. "Since you've got the baby and all, and you've done well where you are, I've got you a church with a brick parsonage, a three-bedroom brick parsonage. The salary's considerably more too. You're going to need more money than you've been making, and you'll only need to move across town."

Well it was a shock and a wonderful surprise at the same time. After Rosalie got home, they took the baby and rode part of the way across Atlanta about twelve to fourteen miles and went to look at the new church with parsonage. Their stay turned out to be a positive growth experience for them and for the church.

The South Bend Methodist Church had a little frame building. It also had a basement behind it that had been built twenty-five to thirty years earlier. They had topped it off with black top and tar after the basement structure had been put in. Then it had simply sat there all those years, and they'd never been able to raise the funds to complete it by putting the upper story over it.

In that first year of Danny's ministry there, the church had a new building built over that basement, and the basement rooms were finished. They had a bond drive, and the building was built before the end of Danny and Rosalie's year there. The people couldn't quite believe it. A common comment was, "After all these years, we're doing what we wanted to do and never have been able to." This made it all the more difficult for Danny to say to them that he was moving on.

He had a friend in Dr. Edwin Hartz, a former professor at FSU in Tallahassee, Florida. Dr. Hartz was chaplain at the university. He said to Danny, "Would you be interested in coming back to Florida?" Danny said, "No," because they were in the building process at South Bend Church and were just about ready to complete their first year. Later his friend called again and said that Dr. Glenn James, senior pastor of Trinity in Tallahassee, wanted him to come be his associate. In fact, he told Danny to prepare for a call from Dr. James.

It so happened that Dr. James had been his pastoral idol for the four years of his university days. He was a preacher's preacher. After Dr. James called, he and Rosalie went down and interviewed. They were offered the job that was really a conference appointment, with Dr. James making the arrangements. It was a tough thing to go to his people back in South Bend and tell them they were leaving in only two weeks.

One reason Danny wanted to go to Trinity was that he had had almost five years of "struggling church" experience, and he wanted to be in a church that was succeeding and achieving. He felt a deep need to have a successful experience after much pulling and pushing, trying to move churches beyond where they were or wanted to be. Trinity was a big, strong church that could do whatever it was satisfied to do.

Soon after arriving in his new appointment to Trinity, he asked Dr. James, "Does it make you nervous to be preaching to high-powered people every Sunday? There is the president of the university, lots of professors, doctors, the governor and several of his cabinet! How do you feel when you preach to them every Sunday?"

Dr. James casually replied, "I feel just as sorry for them as I do for you." That simple reply wiped away Danny's anxiety and helped him realize that people, no matter what their title, were all in need of the Gospel. His concern about important people dissipated as he began to get to know them and minister to them.

He had been working intensely with school, a new family, and ministry. Like most young ministers, he had yet to learn that he must attend his own soul as well as to the souls of others, and dryness set in. Starting out in ministry at the age of nineteen, he had sacrificed and penalized himself by putting his schooling in third place after relationships and church work. Because of that difficult period, he was eager to tell later seminarians, "Don't get a church for the first couple of years you're there. Be a student. You can always get a church. You'll spend forty to fifty years in a church, but you can't always be a student. Get the most you can get out of your studies and being part of that academic community. Then in time, the other will come, and you can handle it better if you get yourself properly prepared."

After two wonderful and challenging years as associate pastor at Trinity, Danny was appointed to start a new church in

Tallahassee. The city had grown by twenty thousand since a Methodist church was started. He was appointed to start the new John Wesley Church that was jointly sponsored by Trinity and St. Paul Methodist churches.

As a result of his double (and triple) duty during his university days, and his increasing load of going to seminary, being a pastor, and new family responsibilities, he was feeling weary more and more of the time. He began to feel spiritually dry. Starting the new church had been exciting and challenging, but draining. After about three years at John Wesley Church, the stress began to take a toll. His inner spirit was not being nourished, and burnout began to be apparent. Because of the spiritual dryness in his life, it became difficult—very difficult—for him to get to the pulpit on Sunday mornings. He found it impossible to prepare adequately. He was drying up inside.

As she watched him struggle, Rosalie anguished over this, seeing how he was diverting his attention, compromising, trying to pour out of a dry cup. She developed a pattern of asking him, "How are you doin' for Sunday?" He would respond, "Okay," but very weakly. The next question was, "Have you worked on your sermon much?" To which he responded even more quietly, "Emmhmm." This was followed by, "Do you think you're ready?" And then the clinker, Danny always knew was coming and dreaded it. "Danny, have you prayed about your sermon?" She never asked antagonistically, but rather plaintively.

One day they were driving, Danny at the wheel, on the edge of the university where he had gone to school. Rosalie started the familiar series of questions. They were both particularly heavy in their spirits that day because he was coming up so flat and so short. He pulled into a parking space because he didn't want to drive and deal with his spiritual despair. They sat there in silence for a while. Then they began talking about it.

He told her how he felt, how tough it was, and what a struggle it was to try to do what he was doing. With discouragement in his voice he confessed, "I feel like I'm called to be a spiritual leader, but I'm not. It just eats me up." Rosalie turned sort of halfway in the seat, put her hand on his knee, and between sobs, said, "Oh, Danny, I feel we're trapped, and there's nothing we can do about it." He confirmed her feelings, and the tears continued for both for some time.

After a while, he said a prayer of commitment, coming up out of that brokenness, that emptiness. He made a new commitment through prayer to ministry and to God to try to be the person God wanted him to be. Then he turned on the ignition, backed up, and pulled out of the parking place. It had been a heart-wrenching time.

He was faithful to that prayer of commitment, and he began to pray and to work harder on his sermons. To his surprise, it made a difference. People began to say, "Who's that preaching? I thought Danny was preaching, but that doesn't sound like him." There was more vigor in his sermons because they were better prepared. There was more *heart* in them.

He went on through the fall feeling like new life was slowly emerging. He went to hear other people preach. He read more; he worked on his sermons. He wanted to make sure they were well prepared and well delivered. At last, he was feeling a spiritual resurgence—more energy, more life. He actually began to like his work.

As he and Rosalie talked one day, they realized they were both thinking what they really needed was a new church to cap off this sense of rebirth. Danny believed that what would really launch him into a new beginning would be a new place, a new group of people, and a new set of problems. He began to pray earnestly, especially for a new appointment.

Several weeks passed. Then early in January, District Superintendent Dr. Robert Holmes called him and said, "Danny, there's a church! Its quite a church! I think you're the person for it. I'm going to a meeting with Bishop Henley and the other district superintendents. We'll be praying and making mid-year appointments. I'll call you."

Danny felt this news was an answer to prayer. He waited for the confirmation, but not a word came. He waited even a couple of days longer without hearing anything, and then his feathers fell because he realized that "no call" meant no good news. Finally, Dr. Holmes returned and called Danny, asking him to come by. Dr. Holmes said, "Well, we had a good cabinet meeting,

and I want to tell you what happened. We put your name down
to go to that church. Your name was put on the official list. We
moved on to consider eight or ten other churches and appointments. On a break, the bishop called me over and said, 'Bob, I
don't know why, but I just have the feeling that this is not the
time for Danny to move. I can't tell you why, but I just don't
think this is the time.' Then we went back and appointed another
person to that church."

Dr. Holmes said he was sorry things hadn't worked out, but
reassured Danny that he had done the best he could to see that
he got a new church. With whipped-up Southern graciousness,
Danny thanked him and told him how much he appreciated his
effort.

It was a crushing disappointment. There was still enough of
a sense of burnout that he didn't know how he was going to
crank up the energy needed to continue where he was. He went
home and told Rosalie. If she wept about it, it was behind closed
doors. He went into a pit of depression. There simply was no
hope he could see to recover and refocus his motivation and
momentum.

On top of all this, in 1960 the civil rights movement was
emerging with sit-ins and marches. There were two universities
in Tallahassee—Florida A & M and Florida State. Florida A & M
was an African-American school, and FSU was an all-white
school. Of course Florida A & M students wanted to change
the status quo, and the university was a tinderbox of racial
activity. There was a two-week period when racial tensions
were very high with innuendoes and rumors piling one upon
another. One rumor was that blacks were being bussed into
town with baseball bats to be used in a demonstration. The
truth was that a black baseball team had come to town for a
game at Florida A & M.

In the midst of the rumors, there was a sit-in at Trinity
Methodist, the large, downtown Methodist church. Dr. Glen
James, the senior pastor, had taken the position that the demon-
strators were welcome. Some members supported the action, but
some were outraged. Still, when they came, they were welcomed
and seated like everyone else.

Members of John Wesley Church wondered what should be done if there was a demonstration there. The church was temporarily meeting in a public school. The chairman of the Leon County School Board had told Danny that the board didn't want to get involved in racial issues in the church. If blacks came and were seated, the board would ask the church to move. It seemed impossible that the church would be able to find space to meet if it was required to move.

Danny anguished over the dilemma. He felt the church was between a rock and a hard place: He wanted John Wesley to be a "real church—one that welcomed all people." But if they took that position, there was a very real possibility the church would have no place to meet.

One night he had a powerful dream. Because of the dream, he sat upright in bed and shouted aloud, "The church must be true to itself!" His pulse was racing because of the intensity of the experience. He instantly knew he had been given the right answer. This dream confirmed his belief that all were one in Jesus Christ.

At a church board meeting the following night, the question came up. He then reported what he had been told by the school board chairman. He said, "If we seat black students, we shall be asked to find another place for the church to meet. We don't know of another space to accommodate us."

He then stated the question, "What shall we do?" He immediately answered by telling his dream of the night before, and then said, "I propose that we welcome and seat whoever comes to our church. If that becomes a problem for anyone, we will deal with that later."

The board affirmed the decision by a unanimous vote, and the question never surfaced again.

As it turned out, there was no demonstration, but a great battle had been won: the John Wesley congregation had chosen to be true to itself as a church—the body of Christ.

CHAPTER THREE

Shaped by Scripture
And Not a Minute Too Soon

Scripture has had a profound and lasting effect on Danny's personal life and on his ministry. In particular, three scripture passages have become metaphors for Danny's ministry. He speaks of these with reverence and power in his own words as follows:

Great value has come to me in identifying biblical metaphors that relate to my experiences. It was not by design that I have selected one metaphor from the Old Testament, one from Psalms, and one from the New Testament. I just stumbled on them. I have lived with these three biblical gifts for a number of years, and they are now truly my own.

I have encouraged many persons to begin a quiet, on-going Bible study searching for a personal biblical metaphor that will be unmistakably and clearly theirs when they find it.

THE OLD TESTAMENT—A FAITH CHALLENGE

My Old Testament metaphor is the story of Elijah and the Baal priests (1 Kings 18:20–39 NRSV). Elijah had become fed up with the fickle people who on one day would be committed to the Lord, and the next day would worship the Baal god. He challenged the Baal priests to what I think of as a contest—a "show-down at high noon."

Elijah asked the Baal priests to go first and build an altar to their god, but instead of putting fire to it, they would call to their

god to send fire upon their altar. Elijah would, in turn, build an
altar and call to the Lord God to send fire from heaven. Then, the
people could watch the results and judge for themselves who was
the greatest—the Lord God or the Baal god.

Elijah announced that he was willing to go with the
people's choice: "If the Lord is God, follow him. But if Baal,
then follow him" (1 Kings 18:21). Dr. Peter Marshall added,
". . . and go to hell."

The Baal priests took the dare and built a great altar. All 450
of them marched, chanted, and called to their god throughout the
morning, "O Baal, answer us! But there was no voice, and no one
answered" (vs. 26). Nothing happened. Nothing!

About noon Elijah began to heckle and kibitz. I can
imagine Elijah sitting under a big tree for shade, chewing on a
stick. Finally, he stood, tossed his stick and said, "What's the
matter? Where is your god? Has he gone on vacation? Is he
asleep" (vs. 27)?

I like old Elijah, but the Baal priests didn't. They became
infuriated and began to shout louder than before and to march
faster. They eventually became serious and desperate enough that
they began cutting their arms with knives and spears trying to get
their god's attention. They kept it up, but no fire fell.

I imagine it was probably about 5:30 in the afternoon. Elijah
stood, stretched, held up his arms and shouted, "You've had your
chance, now it is my time." Motioning to those nearby, he said,
"Build an altar of twelve large stones and put on it twelve large
pieces of wood, and put the sacrificial meat upon the wood on
the altar." Then he made a deep trench around the altar and
commanded them to pour four barrels of water on the altar. (I
silently think—*That is just like my man, Elijah—gutsy!*)

Then Elijah said, "Pour on four more barrels of water!" I
almost want to pull Elijah off to the side and say, "I've tried to
burn wet wood. I think you have more than made your point
with the first four barrels."

Then Elijah said, "Pour on four more barrels of water," and
I throw up my hands and back away, shaking my head. The Bible
says, "The water ran all around the altar, and filled the trench
also with water" (vs. 35).

Now both the people and the Baal priests stood with opened mouths. Elijah backed away from the altar a few steps, lifted his face toward the heavens and in a loud voice shouted, "O Lord God of Israel, let it be known this day that you are God in Israel, that I am your servant, and that I have done all these things at your bidding" (vs. 36). "Then the fire of the Lord fell and consumed the burnt offering, the wood, the stones and the dust and even licked up the water that was in the trench" (vs. 38). When all the people saw it, they fell on their faces, and said, "The Lord indeed is God, the Lord indeed is God" (vs. 39).

I see this story illustrating the first years of my ministry when I had only a strong ethical orientation for ministry. Late one afternoon something happened that gave me a completely new spiritual orientation.

Our family was camping in the Smokies one summer while our three children were small. They wanted a campfire on a rainy afternoon. With odds against me, I tried unsuccessfully to start a fire with wet oak wood.

"Please, Daddy, try to hurry. Can't we have a little fire? We are cold!"

At the last I was sitting there in a wet raincoat and drenched, with my last gofer match in my hand—you know, you strike one and gofer another. Finally, no more matches and no fire. I sat there shining my flashlight on a wet pile of wood. And it was like I was transfixed by what I saw. I did not want to move.

Rosalie came out of the camper. She was warm and wearing a dry raincoat. She just watched me sitting there shining my flashlight on that woodpile. Finally, she said softly, "What are you doing?"

I said, "I'm shining this flashlight on this woodpile."

Another pause. "Do you think you can get the wood to burn that way?" I said, "Dear, you probably ought to get back inside the camper!"

She left me sitting there shining the light on the woodpile. I thought, "I will *never* get this fire started this way. All I have is *light*. What I want is *fire*."

I can't say how long I sat there, arrested by what I saw and by what I was thinking. I thought, "This is how my ministry has been all these years. Just as tonight I have light, and what I need

is fire, that is the way it has been in my ministry. All I have had
is the light of Jesus' teachings; as wonderful as that light is, it is
not enough. I need fire on this woodpile, and I need fire in my
ministry—and I don't have either. I don't have either!"

When Elijah called for the fire of heaven to fall upon his altar,
it was not the Baal god, it was Elijah's God—*no, it was my God*—
who sent the fire of heaven. And it is my God who must send the
fire of heaven upon the altar of my heart, and upon the altar of our
church, and upon the altar of the hearts of our people back home.
This is the work of the Holy Spirit. Later, I discovered that in the
New Testament, the power of the Holy Spirit is referred to some
three hundred times as *dunamis* in Greek—our word for dynamite.

And suddenly, the astounding vision was complete. For the first
time, I realized that as grand as they are, it is not *enough* for me to
walk in the light of the teachings of Jesus—because Jesus brought
more than His teachings. He also brought the Holy Spirit!

I must have light *and* fire!

*I must walk through the light of the teachings of Jesus—walk
on through the light into the fire of the Holy Spirit.*

That's it! The light of Jesus' teachings illumines the path for
my journey. Then, the Holy Spirit comes like spiritual dynamite
and brings the fire of heaven that cleanses and purifies, and
tempers my soul as fire tempers steel. Fire provides power, spiritual energy—precisely what I didn't have. In every generation the
church has had light, but in a few generations it has also had fire!
Only God sends fire—on Elijah's altar, and ours!

My prayer became, "Come Holy Spirit. Bring the fire of
heaven upon the altar of my heart!" My ministry began to receive
a new direction, a new power, and a new thrust. I would never be
the same again!

THE PSALM—INSIGHTS FOR THE TOUGH TIMES

Another passage that helps my life and ministry is taken from
Psalm 30:10–12 NRSV, which is my favorite psalm.

Lord, you heard, and were gracious to me;
O Lord, you were my helper.

You turned my grief into dancing.
Stripped me of sorrow and clothed me with joy.
So my heart will sing to you; not weep;
Lord, my God, I will praise you forever.

The psalm speaks almost too directly to me at various points:

You brought me up from the grave;
You restored me to life from among the dead (vs. 3).

The car accident I had on a laid-back Saturday afternoon brought these verses to mean a great deal to me. I do not know how close I actually came to the grave. I only know it was so close, I am threatened to tears when I ponder the circumstances. Fifteen years later, all is better, but I had a close call. Yes, this is my psalm! "We weep in the evening, but laugh at dawn" (vs. 5).

I have no memory of the accident or the first five hours that followed. I was not unconscious, but was constantly talking, asking over and over again if our little dog, Ruggy, was hurt. Ruggy had not even been in the car with me. My family was standing by my bed laughing when I came to consciousness again. Their laughter was the nervous kind that reflected their relief that I was still with them. I was assured that Ruggy had not gotten his haircut that day and was home doing okay. Apart from the five-hour period of memory loss and the terrific headache, I appeared to be doing fine, and I left the hospital in only three days. I had a pleasant three-week recuperation with very little pain.

The heavy time of five hours of that frightening evening had quickly turned to laughter. This is my psalm!

What will you gain if I died in tears (vs. 9)?

I shudder to recall how close to me that question had come. I now read with awe, the following powerful sentences of experienced providence:

Lord, you heard, and were gracious to me;
O Lord, you were my helper.

You turned my grief into dancing.
Stripped me of sorrow and clothed me with joy (vs. 11).

Those words are exact expressions of my deepest feelings, and they always move me to heartfelt thanksgiving.

So my heart will sing to you, not weep,
Lord, my God, I will praise you forever (vs. 12).

I can never fully explain how beneficial it has been to discover a psalm that so profoundly parallels my experience and expresses my joy. (Verse translation from *The Psalms: A New Translation for Prayer and Worship*, by Gary Chamberlain.)

THE NEW TESTAMENT—THE WOMAN IN THE CROWD

I recall one particular Bible story that I began to see as a New Testament metaphor for my life. That metaphor is the woman with the issue of blood for twelve years in Mark 5:25–34 RSV.

The woman was in the crowd, following after Jesus for a personal reason—she wished to be healed. She had lived with hemorrhages for twelve years. She came up behind Jesus getting closer and closer to him. She held a strong conviction, "If I but touch his clothes, I will be made well" (vs. 28). The moment came when she acted on that marvelous expectation, "And she touched his cloak" (vs. 27).

Immediately aware that power had gone forth from him, Jesus turned about in the crowd and asked, "Who touched me" (vs. 30)?

And the woman was immediately healed. What a marvelous biblical story! But it has become more than just a biblical story for me—it is a metaphor for the progressive stages of my spiritual journey.

Being a Casual Christian

For several years after I became a Christian, I was much like the woman, just following Jesus "as one of the crowd." And like the woman, I too was broken and in need of healing, but for a different reason. My close identity was not with her condition, but with her plight. Although I was committed to Christ and his service, I was spiritually dry and empty, probably because I was only a *casual Christian*, even if I was working at it full time. Having been called to be a spiritual leader, I was nowhere near fulfilling that call. At that time I characterized myself as being a casual Christian, and I now label that as the beginning stage of my spirituality.

Being a Seeker Christian

For a while the woman stopped short of making the forward movement to actually touch Jesus. She *knew* that Jesus had the power to effect a healing change in her condition. She held no question that Jesus could do it, but she held back.

Like this woman, early on I was perhaps a *seeker Christian*, in that I *knew* there was a transforming power in Jesus, but I had never experienced it. It is one thing to know of that power and quite another thing to actually experience it. I knew where the power was, and I realized that my transformation was possible. But for a long time, I simply continued to hold that knowledge in my head.

I recall moving on to become a seeker after Christ himself, and it made all the difference in me. It is like I could know there is a cool, clear, and refreshing spring up ahead, but it does not refresh unless I actually drink from the spring. For quite a while I knew that Jesus had the power, but I was content to only hold that knowledge and not act to experience Jesus' power.

That knowledge is what characterizes a seeker Christian, the conviction that Jesus has the power to change one's life, to heal, to save, to redeem one's whole life. That is one's motivation for "seeking after. . . ."

We wouldn't have this biblical story if the woman had remained content to simply be a *casual Christian* in the crowd, or satisfied with her head knowledge about Jesus' transforming power. She acted! She took another step, and she touched him. She touched him, and she was instantly healed. With that decisive, life-changing action, she made a big move forward and became a *radical Christian*.

Being a Radical Christian

The word *radical* does not mean wild-eyed, bizarre, frenzied, off-the-wall, or strange. Having radical surgery does not mean surgery that is massive or dramatic or necessarily life threatening. The word *radical* means *original*. Radical surgery is done to restore as near as possible the original state of wellness.

The woman became a *radical Christian* because by touching Jesus, she got in touch with the *original source* of spiritual power, and it was healing and life-transforming power.

This part of the woman's story is definitely my story! This touching! It has happened many times in my life. Getting close enough to Jesus to touch his original source of power is the only explanation I have for the power for family life, for ministry in general, for preaching in particular, for overcoming burnout, or for simply surviving in a day like ours. The power comes from being close to Jesus, touching Jesus. The Holy Spirit comes into our lives as surely as it entered into the woman that day, when we are *close enough to Jesus to touch. To be close enough to Jesus to touch* is to love him, to follow him, and to be an incarnation of his Spirit as much as possible.

When I fail to be close enough to Jesus to touch, when I am content only to know that touching is possible but stop short of actually experiencing Jesus' *radical power*, I am in trouble. (I got into this kind of trouble five or six years after I entered the ministry.) I am left in my own brokenness, and I lack the spiritual power that I require. I am of all people, most miserable.

This story has also become the metaphor for my ministry as well as my life (as if the two were separate). I am continuously energized by the hope and possibility of helping others make that ultimate movement to become *radical Christians*. I delight to see Christians who may have been *casual followers* of Jesus in the crowd move forward to become seekers who hold the knowledge that Jesus can transform them. But my greatest delight in ministry is to see a person move from head knowledge about Jesus to personal experience of Jesus. For several years that has been my hope and my greatest joy—to see the church increasingly filled with *radical Christians*.

CHAPTER FOUR

The Great Experiment

"On the right path,
the limping foot recovers strength
and does not collapse."—Heb. 12:13 PHILLIPS

While Danny languished in a kind of apathy and spiritual depression, his fishing partner, Sam Teague, was about to be visited by inspiration. Sam was a member of the new church, a banker, a state senator, and the mayor of Florida's capital city. Sam sought solitude at his office early on Sunday mornings to pray and review his preparations for teaching the Christian Homebuilders, the young adult class he taught at John Wesley Church. He was a popular teacher with these under-thirty-five-year-old adults. He prepared his own curriculum. In the summer he took a sabbatical from teaching to prepare his lessons for the other nine months of the year.

On what came to be a remarkable Sunday morning, January 24, 1965, Sam let himself into his office at the Leon Federal Savings and Loan Association to get ready for his class. After spending some time in prayer and reflection, he looked up at the clock. It said nine o'clock; it was time to go. He put his things in his briefcase and started to rise, when a disquieting thought came to him: "What's the use of going out there and talking to them? I can't see any difference after teaching for two years. They're like plastic people. Many are so empty and don't even know it. They just sit there and listen, drink it up, pick up their children and go home." All of them were well educated—some were government employees, people in leadership, many with their own businesses.

With the feeling of futility in what he was trying to do as their teacher and their lack of response, Sam put his head down on his desk, and in an anguished prayer, he prayed, "O God, show me how to challenge these young people so they can have a life that matters!" (It was about a fifteen-second prayer if you pray it right.)

As Sam started to rise, a thought came to him. He had a pad there, so he wrote it down. Before he finished writing, another thought and another came. He kept writing.

As the writing continued, he recorded many thoughts. Suddenly, he had a sense that his hand *was being written through*. It was some power greater than he was that was at work through him. He had never thought of these ideas that were pouring forth. He had never talked about them to anyone, nor had he read them anywhere. Sam's consciousness was simply flooded with inspiration. The chill bumps stood up on his arms. He continued to write, turning page upon page. The more he wrote, the greater the sense of inspiration. At one point, the *presence* was so great that he turned around to see if someone was standing behind him.

Finally, like that, the river went dry. All the inspiration stopped. There was not another thought to record. It was over. He breathed a deep, releasing sigh. Looking at the clock again, he noted only twenty minutes had passed, twenty minutes to write God's answer to that fifteen-second prayer.

Sam went to class that day, but didn't say a word about what had happened. The significance of what took place simply hadn't sunk in yet. The next morning, as was often his custom, Danny went by Sam's office to see if he was free for coffee or to have breakfast.

As it happened, Sam did want to have breakfast. They went next door to their usual coffee shop. As they waited for their food to arrive, Sam pulled a piece of paper from his pocket and asked Danny to take a look at it. On the card his secretary had typed the challenge, "Wanted Ten Brave Christians," together with a list of spiritual disciplines to be practiced for a month:

1. Meet once each week to pray together.
2. Give two hours' time each week to the church.
3. Give God one-tenth of our earnings.
4. Spend 5:30–6:00 each morning in prayer and meditation.
5. Witness for God our experience to others.

Danny looked at it and said, "Hmmm, where did you get this?" Sam casually replied, "I'll tell you sometime. What do you think about it?"

Danny looked at the card again and suddenly became very uncomfortable because he was the only pastor John Wesley Church ever had. The church was five years old now and had taken in over 450 members. He read the five disciplines again and a sense of threat came because he very quickly concluded that they wouldn't find ten people who would do those five things. He was their spiritual leader. If they couldn't find ten, it would be an indictment against the church and his spiritual leadership. Sitting there in silence he felt more threatened than he'd ever been in his life.

Sam remained quiet. He just let Danny sit there. He had no idea what Danny was processing so intensely. Danny's first response was to ask, "Sam, you aren't planning to do this in our church are you?"

Sam asked, "Well, what do you think?"

Danny continued to look at the paper, still feeling terribly anxious. Actually, little time went by, yet his whole life and ministry began unraveling within him. He thought, "I've not been the kind of preacher who would call people like this into the church. I've been a popular preacher, hail-fellow-well-met, full of optimism with a synthetic Norman Vincent Peale-ism that would make Dr. Peale nauseated, talking a good game, making people feel good, telling them what they want to hear, being optimistic. Yes, always being optimistic."

He remembers thinking, "Jesus called the church the body of Christ. That's what the church is supposed to be." But that is not the kind of church we were. He had recently read that Victor Hugo described the church as "an anvil that has worn out many hammers," but he realized that didn't describe John Wesley Church. He did think that the church should be that way though. A sense of the rightness of it began to move into his thoughts.

The simple challenge was to put God first!

In little more than a twinkling of an eye, he began to take courage. He began to say to himself, "This is the right way to do this, a new way for me."

The Challenge to Put God First

WANTED: TEN BRAVE CHRISTIANS

Who for one month:

1. Will meet once each week to pray together.
2. Will give two hours time each week to God. (Self-surrender)
3. Will give God one-tenth of earnings during this month. (Self-denial)
4. Will spend 5:30–6:00 each morning in prayer and meditation. (Self-control)
5. Will witness for God their experience to others.

Study these five principles carefully so that there is no misunderstanding as to what is involved in surrendering your life to God. Here is the commitment you make now:

> To prepare my life to receive from God the great strength and power available through prayer, I ask to be a member of this prayer group.

He summoned up uncommon courage, leaned forward in his seat, looked Sam right in the eye and said, "Let's see if we can find ten people who will put God first in their lives. If we can, it will blow the lid off this church. If we can't, I'll have something to preach about the rest of my life."

Here began a powerful spiritual whirlwind that profoundly affected Danny and Rosalie, Sam and John Wesley Church, and countless others.

The story related here is about the "John Wesley Great Experiment" as they first began to call it. That was an appropriate title for the new small-group emphasis. It was an experiment because they had no idea what would happen as they began to "put God first" in the practice of these five disciplines. It started in John Wesley Church.

Across the years the challenge has affectionately been known in various places by several titles: *the Great Experiment*; *The John Wesley Great Experiment*; *The Brave Christian Program*; "Wanted: Ten Brave Christians"; and *The Brave Christian Movement* (because it eventually became a movement in the United Methodist Church and beyond).

※ ※ ※

In 1999 the book *A Life That Really Matters* was rewritten with its face to the future. The title was kept, but the new book is about 85 percent new content. The General Commission of United Methodist Men adopted this challenge as their spiritual formation program for 2001 and beyond. At that point in time, *The John Wesley Great Experiment* booklet was restyled with the new title, *The Wesley Experience*. (After more than thirty-five years this is no longer an experiment—it is an experience, a *spiritual experience*, somewhat like Mr. Wesley had.)

For simplicity, in this book we have selected the name the "Great Experiment" to refer to the *historical* development of the challenge.

For the next six weeks, both Sam and Danny put all their energies into calling people to put God first in their lives; Sam in his class for those twenty-one to thirty-five years of age and Danny from the pulpit. Momentum of the challenge to put God first was building. Near the end of the challenge period, Danny preached on the text from Hebrews 12:13 PHILLIPS, "On the right path, the limping foot recovers strength and does not collapse." He knew what it was like to be a limping foot, and he felt that the Great Experiment was the right path.

Finally the day came to see if there were any takers. To their surprise, twenty-two people responded. That group met the month of March 1965. They gave another invitation in April when sixteen more people responded, a total of thirty-eight people in just a two-month period. In many ways, it blew the lid off the church just as predicted.

Here is a bird's eye view of the heart of the challange. There is more to it, but his is the heart of it.

The following guidelines are for how to spend the thirty
minutes on prayer and meditation from 5:30 to 6:00 each morning:

5:30–5:40 Read Scripture for the day (see schedule). Pray and
meditate on this Scripture. Write out in less than fifty words
and in less than ten minutes what the passage says to you.

5:40–5:50 Write out one totally unselfish and unexpected act of
kindness or generosity you will do today. Name the person and
name the deed—then act during the day, vigorously and with
love and compassion. Keep a written record of (1) the reaction
of the person toward whom the kindness is extended and (2)
the effect of this act upon you personally.

5:50–6:00 Write out carefully how you would like to build and
develop your life. Go into great detail if you desire. Take your
time—be thoughtful and prayerful. One well prayed-out and
thought-out sentence per day would be excellent progress.

Here is Danny's commentary on the three ten-minute
segments:

1. The first ten-minute period is a reflection on Scripture—
   how it *ought* to be in our lives.
2. In the second ten minutes we were discovering how it *really*
   is with us. This second component was the most difficult part
   of the entire challenge. The good deed was to be something
   one was not obligated to do, or paid to do. This was relatively easy for the first four or five days, but then we began
   to struggle because using these criteria for selection made it
   difficult to select even one good deed to do for just one
   person in an entire day. We began to sense that we were
   innately and profoundly ingrown and self-centered. To begin
   to reverse that pattern is like unto a conversion experience.

Often, there was a powerfully disturbing dynamism of miss-
match between the two. That discovery set the stage for our
deeper reflections in the third ten minutes: . . . how do you want

Scripture Readings for the First Four Months

FIRST MONTH

The passages for the first month were carefully selected and arranged in a rhythmic pattern. One passage may challenge, the next may affirm, the next may comfort, and the next may arouse. Together, they provide a unique personal invitation to put God first.

Day 1	2 Chron. 7:14	Day 17	Isa. 59:1–3
2	James 4:16	18	Prov. 28:9–10
3	1 John 1:9	19	Matt. 8:24–27
4	John 15:6–7	20	John 6:47
5	Mark 11:24	21	Eccles. 8:1–8
6	Phil. 4:6	22	Ps. 55:22
7	1 John 5:14	23	John 14:27
8	Jer. 29:13	24	Psalms 1:1–8
9	Matt. 6:7–13	25	John 14:1
10	Matt. 18:19	26	Matt. 6:25–33
11	Isa. 65:23–24	27	Ps. 23:1–6
12	Matt. 6:6	28	Mark 12:30
13	Luke 11:9–10	29	Heb. 12:1
14	Isa. 58:9–11	30	John 4:14
15	Ps. 127:1	31	Matt. 5:13–16
16	Ps. 66:18		

to build and develop your life? When you get to the end and look back, what do you want to be *known* for? Because of the first two, this third segment of the daily spiritual exercise began to take on deeper and deeper significance.

Scripture Readings

During a six-week period Sam surveyed three hundred passages with a concordance and selected thirty-one. The passages are brief—mostly one to three verses. He carefully arranged them in a wavelike pattern so that they had a rhythmic impact. One passage may challenge, the next may affirm, the next may comfort, and the next may arouse.

Together, they provide a unique personal invitation to put God first. (There are four months of Scripture selections.)

This spiritual experiment was the beginning of all kinds of firsts for Sam and Danny. They went to their first small group meeting and were its leaders. After the first meeting, they realized that there were too many for one group, so they divided. At the second meeting, eleven people met from 6:30–8:00 P.M. and another eleven from 8:30–10:00 P.M.

On the following Sunday, three of the group walked up and said, "Sam, Danny, we don't want to meet in two groups anymore. All of us are meeting together this week in case you would like to join us." Sam and Danny chuckled and were delighted to see such interest and vitality. Throughout both months they practiced the five disciplines Sam had written down that memorable morning.

Sam and Danny went to the meetings and led them as a team. Neither one knew what they were doing because small groups were entirely new to both. They got some tracts on small groups from the Yokefellow Institute. This helped them realize that meetings ought not to be too long. Everyone ought to get a chance to talk. And there needed to be a prayer time. That was about all they knew, and they felt good that some of those principles were already part of the Great Experiment challenge. Many people's personal and spiritual lives began to experience revolutionary change, including Danny's and Rosalie's. They were astounded! It was obviously nothing they were doing, but the Spirit was moving deeply. Fully three-fourths of those two groups underwent profound spiritual changes in that two-month period. All were significantly impacted. Love, spiritual energy, excitement, and answered prayer characterized every weekly meeting. There were only two absences over the five Tuesday nights of the first month. Danny had never known a church could be like this!

It elevated the ministry of John Wesley Church from the doldrums to vitality, purpose, and spiritual integrity. This was a totally new experience for Danny. He had felt personal, spiritual vitality at times before, but had never known it in a pastoral role.

His friend, Sam, who was a very spiritually mature person, was a tremendous mentor for Danny. Sam was not trying to teach him something. He was guiding Danny from deep spiritual insight that came from a mature common sense and wisdom, the result of Sam's prayer life. He was being led by the Holy Spirit and was given new insights and directions for the journey he and Danny were on as leaders. Danny learned more from this experience about how to be a pastor and how a church could be a *real* church than from all of his prior years of ministry put together. He and Sam learned much down in the trenches as they tried to guide and survive the avalanche of new life in the church.

Two major discoveries Danny made were the power of the laity and the power of the Holy Spirit. He was not familiar with either. The lay people agreed to sign up to work in the church two hours a week for four weeks. It doesn't sound like much, but there were twenty-two people, giving forty-four hours of service per week, in a church of about five hundred members. They did it for four weeks, with sixteen more people giving thirty-two hours of service per week in April, with all of the first group continuing (you do the math). It was like a space shuttle launch at Cape Kennedy. When they said, "Yes, I'll be in this group," they stepped up on the rocket pad and the Holy Spirit lifted them into orbit in ministry in some very dramatic ways. Many had life-changing experiences.

In his early ministry, Danny was purposely reluctant to relate to the Holy Spirit in a personal way. Throughout childhood he had been associated with people who were very conservative theologically and were religiously demonstrative. They claimed that they did everything *on the authority of the Holy Spirit*. These ways were not his ways. Early on, he decided that if the Holy Spirit caused people to act like that, he didn't want anything to do with the Holy Spirit.

During his burning out years, he was comfortable in relating to the Holy Spirit theologically and doctrinally, but not experientially. He was afraid he would go off the deep end if he relented his defensive position. He says it is no wonder that deliberately shying away from the Holy Spirit almost caused him to dry up spiritually in his early years of ministry.

After a dozen years from beginning his ministry, he was discovering that the Holy Spirit is a gentle Spirit, never pushy, never embarrassing, never overbearing. The Holy Spirit can always be trusted. What a shift of consciousness! What a recovery of loss! What a new source of power for doing ministry, loving it, and growing spiritually *in* it!

Danny looks back now and is awed by God's providence. His superintendent had wanted him to move to a bigger church, and he had wanted to move. Yet when the bishop had a hunch it wasn't the right time, the superintendent had had a feeling he was right.

The irony is that if Danny had moved to a church in a new location, he would have moved within two weeks. He would have left the Thursday morning just before Sam received his inspiration on the following Sunday morning. The Great Experiment set the fulcrum of his ministry from then on, and he almost missed it. He would have missed the reshaping of his own spiritual life and what it meant to be a pastor. He would have missed the whole sense of the power of the laity, the presence of the Holy Spirit, and the understanding of the church as the body of Christ.

It had been a hard lesson—to accept the hierarchy's decision that he was not to move. Now Danny realized how God could move through those in authority to facilitate God's will in his life.

The Great Experiment program transformed Danny's life, John Wesley Methodist Church, and his ministry in that church. It wasn't long before he realized he had a *new church* after all, and he didn't even have the expense of having to move. He was new, and the church was new.

Within the first month, he began to get a sense that a quiet movement had started. At John Wesley they began to get invitations for people to go to other churches and tell what was happening. They sent three people to Panama City, Florida, one hundred miles away, to speak at an Episcopal church. Also during that month, Danny was preaching a revival in Tampa, Florida, 250 miles away. On a weekday, five people from the Great Experiment prayer group took off from work and drove the 250 miles to support their pastor, also hoping there might be an opportunity to speak about what was happening at John Wesley Church. He made sure they had that opportunity.

Things began to mushroom. A Baptist preacher in Tallahassee called Danny one day, "I've been hearing what's happening in your church. It's wonderful! What do you call it?" Danny told him, "We sometimes call it the John Wesley Great

Experiment." He replied, "Well, you know the Baptist church. People are kind of funny about other churches and other denominations. I don't know how that would go in our church." Danny, who wasn't possessive of the idea, suggested they "call it 'The John the Baptist Great Experiment,' and it'll go real well." The Baptist preacher said he'd give that a try. So the pastor took the materials, but put out his own brochures called the John the Baptist Great Experiment.

An Episcopal priest across town called. Danny knew him well. He was older, but not by much. He asked, "I've really been excited about what's happening over there at John Wesley. What do you call it?" Danny told him it was "The John Wesley Great Experiment." Again, he received a reply indicating that title might not go in the Episcopal Church. Danny reminded him that John Wesley was an Episcopalian all his life, a member of the Church of England. "With 'John Wesley' you're better off than we are." The priest bought the books and started the Great Experiment in that church.

Danny's ministry took on an expanded sphere of influence beyond its Methodist borders. This foreshadowed a major transition ahead.

In order to see the kind of work the Holy Spirit was doing in the church, we need to look at one of those changed lives. Probably no one better represents the profound changes that were taking place in many people's lives than Happy Woodham. This is his story in his own words.

▦ ▦ ▦

I met Danny back in '61, I reckon. He was assistant pastor at Trinity, a big Methodist church in town. They were plannin' on openin' a new church in a new subdivision where we lived. Danny was goin' to be in charge of it.

One Tuesday night, he was out scoutin' the neighborhood, see'n if they could get members for this new church. My wife and daughter were out, uptown maybe. They didn't want to have much to do with me, I'll tell ya. My recreation after I got home from work was to get drunk, and that's what I was doin'.

I was sittin' there with my drink when the doorbell rang. I went and peeked out the winder and this "fussy-gutted" man was standing there. I had no earthly idea who he was. But I quickly hid my drink in the oven, opened the door and let him in. He introduced himself. Told me what he was after. I said, "Well, I think this is a good idea." However, I was just drunk enough at the time to start arguing theology with him. I could tell by Danny's face that he was thinking, "Man, I wish somebody else had got this name."

We talked on and on. Finally I told him, "Well, listen, I'll make a deal with you. If you will call me on Saturday night and remind me to go to church, I'll start goin' until I make a habit out of it."

Then, he surprised me. He said, "I am not excited about your getting in a habit right now. I just want you to start coming."

I thought I'd given him a pretty good deal. He got up and left. I said, "Well, I got rid of that one fast."

The following Saturday night he called me and said, "I'm goin' to be lookin' for you."

I reckon we did that for a month, month and a half. Finally I told him, "Danny, I don't think you need to call me any more. I believe we've got it lined up now." Rose and Peggy were goin' with me, and we were meetin' in the school house near our home. After we started goin' we met there about a year while they were building the church.

I'll be honest with ya, I wasn't any better a Christian than I was before I met Danny, but I went to church because it was good for business. I could manage to stay sober long enough to get through church, but whenever I'd leave church, I'd drive by a little ole mini market. I'd go in there and get me a couple o' six packs of beer and come home, sit down and start watchin' a ball game. Usually, I wouldn't know when the sun went down.

But I was there every Sunday morning. They put me on the board of the church. I ushered and all of that good stuff. I wouldn't give you a nickle a dozen for every Christian that walked through there. But, I was one of them. And you know, they all thought I was a Christian.

In fact in Sunday school one morning, I told about drinkin'. I was sittin' next to this lady and she says, "I don't know how they expect us to help these alcoholics if we can't get 'em to church." I chuckled to myself, "Lady, if you only knew who was sittin' next to you." She thought everybody who had a drinking problem had to be down on skid row.

A few years down the road, I guess it was in 1965, they started the Ten Brave Christians program. Sam Teague started it up in his Sunday school class. At the end of the first month, they had this group get up and witness in church. I was there, ushering, getting people in, pattin' them on the back. (I'd been drunk up until two o'clock that mornin'.)

I was standin' just outside the back door, and they were up there talkin'. I figured what they were saying was some rot. Then a young woman got up and she started talkin', pretty young lady. She started talkin' about how she used to run around and how she drank before she got into the Ten Brave Christian Program. My first reaction was, "My God, why didn't I meet you back then?"

I went inside and sat down on the back row. They finally got through talkin'. I said to myself, "Well now, if the Lord can do that for her, why can't he do it for me?"

I started arguing with the devil. The members of the first Ten Brave Christians group asked if anybody would come up and be in a second group in April. Rose was sittin' on the front row. She didn't even walk up there; she crawled. I thought, "Oh my God, now Rose is goin' to get religion, I'm goin' home and get drunk, and there's goin' to be hell to pay around our house."

The devil had me by the seat of my britches, and the Lord had me by the hair of my head. And praise the Lord, the Lord had a better hold. I'll tell you right now, the hardest thing that I've ever had to do was stand up there that mornin'. But when I stood up and started walkin' down to the front, the closer I got, the easier it got. I can see why Billy Graham says that if people will come forward, there's something about comin' forward that adds someth'n to the commitment. I can understand that, cause when I walked down there that Sunday morning, I didn't know what was gonna' happen. Lookin' around, I was thinking about these people sittin' in the pews, "You're my witnesses now that I'm goin' down front in front of everybody and cry."

I went and knelt down at the altar. I had no idea how to pray. My mom had taught me, "Now I lay me down to sleep," and "Lord, thank you for breakfast." But I knew that just didn't fit in this particular place. So I'll tell you what I prayed. I call this a sinner's prayer, "I said, Lord, I don't know what you've got to offer, but I'm goin' to trade me for it. And I'll guarantee you, you're gonna' come out on the short end of the stick." That was the first prayer that came right from the inside of my bein'.

When I prayed that, lightnin' didn't flash, thunder didn't roll, or curtains didn't split, or nothin'. I can't explain it, but when I prayed, Jesus jumped on that like a duck on a June bug and I knew, I mean, I *knew* that minute that every sin in my life I'd committed was forgiven. I knew that if I dropped dead right then, my spirit would be in heaven before I hit the floor. Now I knew that, but I couldn't explain it. I'm sure as Danny and Sam looked the crowd over and saw me, they thought, "Well there's one that won't stick."

I started home, gettin' close to that little mini market. My car had been stoppin' there so much it'd just turn in by itself. Before I got there, a little voice started sayin' to me, "Give me a chance. Give me a chance." And the first thing ya' know I passed it. I got home, and I didn't get drunk that day. But I did the next night. I fought it a long time, that drinkin'. I tapered off, tapered off, and finally I gave it up.

Well, I joined the program of the John Wesley Great Experiment. The hardest thing for me was to witness what God had done. Even in college, I couldn't stand up and speak before two people. If I walked along the street and saw two people on the other side whisperin', lookin' at me, I'd swear they were talkin' about me. I was that sensitive and insecure. But I said I'd try.

They sent me out to a little church, three of us. I sat there hopin' a big thunderstorm with lightin' would strike the church or something else would happen so I wouldn't have to get up there. I really was scared out of my wits. Well, I did get up and said a silent prayer, "Lord, you're the one that got me here, and now if you don't know what to do with me, we're in trouble."

The Lord surrounded me and filled me with his Spirit, as if he had dropped a "ball jar" over me. Because I had somethin' to say for the first time in my life, I managed to choke it out. Well that was the beginning of my involvement in Lay Witness Missions. The Lord let me go all the way from the tip of Florida to Iowa witnessin'. It's plumb amazing.

Well, then, I started drinkin' again. An invitation came to speak at the North Carolina Conference of the Methodist Church. They were having a meeting at Lake Junaluska. I was having a battle with the bottle. My wife and daughter had gone somewhere, and there wasn't anybody here except me and the Lord. I was sittin' at the table, and the Lord started talkin' to me. Well, I don't know if you ever heard the Lord talk to you. You know he can get to the point right now. You talk to one of your friends, and they'll invent stuff for you around and about, but I mean the Lord just comes right to the point.

"Happy, I think we ought to have a little discussion here. Now if you think I'm goin' to start runnin' interference for you and your drinkin' you're mistaken. You can forget it. I will not take this taste of liquor away from you. You won't be able to stop yourself, but the two of us workin' together, we can handle it. And I'll tell you another thing, you're goin' to Junaluska to speak next weekend, but you're goin' one of two ways—you're either goin' without me or you're goin' with me. If you go with me, I'll bless you all the way."

I went to Junaluska, and I was blessed. That Ten Brave Christians Program got me witnessing to what God had done. Here I was, speakin' to about fourteen hundred people and lovin' it!

CHAPTER FIVE

The Gift of a Mentor
Walking a Stretch Together

Turning back to Danny, let's see how key mentors nudged him in the direction of God's will for his life. One of the means God uses to facilitate ministry is the providential provision of mentors. Mentors are those who have the capacity and the heart to see potential and empower it in others. For Danny, James W. Sells was a key mentoring leader.

Dr. Sells was prominent in the denomination. He was the executive secretary of the Southeastern Jurisdiction, a pioneer, a spiritual innovator, and a leader who empowered others. He was speaking one Saturday at a church only twenty-five miles from Tallahassee.

Danny went over, not expecting anything surprising to occur. When the session concluded, and on the spur of the moment, Danny went up and told Dr. Sells what was happening at John Wesley Church. To Danny's amazement, Dr. Sells indicated that he and his wife, Vera, would like to come and worship there the next day.

On Sunday morning, Dr. and Mrs. Sells arrived. He had a pad and pen to take notes on what he was sensing and feeling. He immediately recognized something dramatic was happening at John Wesley. Among the events he attended was Sam Teague's Sunday school class. He was tremendously moved by what he saw happening, how authentic it was, the spiritual power, and the possibilities.

A major turning point of Danny's spiritual life took place when Dr. Sells was preaching on that Sunday morning and evening. After Dr. Sells preached powerfully on Sunday morning, a man answered the altar call and was obviously involved in a deep spiritual conversion. He was moved to tears as he came forward. Later, Danny suggested that he and Jim follow the man home and talk with him. Jim said, "No, he needs time alone and with his family. You will have plenty of time to see him." This was the first of many conversions. Danny had much to learn about such movements of the Spirit in people's lives.

At the evening service, Dr. Sells was also preaching. When he gave an altar call, Danny responded as a member of the congregation. He knelt at the chancel railing for prayer and tears began to come. After a bit, Dr. Sells asked Danny to pray the benediction. With tears flowing, Danny prayed in general and ended by praying a confession: "O God, I have played the fool in trying to be the kind of preacher I have been." He had thought this at breakfast with Sam a few weeks earlier, but this time it was confessed for all present to hear (but it was nothing new for the people or for God). A major reorientation began at that breakfast meeting and was consummated at the altar of the church that evening. Nothing would ever be the same again for Danny or for John Wesley Church. He said, "I was converted in my own church!"

Dr. and Mrs. Sells spent the night in a hotel, and the next day he said, "Danny, something is happening here that is very unusual. I don't see this very often. You need to write it up. Write up everything that happens on a day-to-day basis. Journal it. You really ought to write a book about what's happening here."

Danny did a double take, "A book?"

"Yes," he said, "this would make a book if it's done right. If you'll write it, I'll publish it. I've got an editor I can give it to, and the editor can polish it. Get it to me even in rough draft form. Don't spend a lot of time, just get the data and the detail, especially the stories of people's lives."

Dr. Sells went on to say that he would send Al Weston, a spiritual life researcher on his staff, to do further exploration and offer counsel. He later encouraged a visit by Ben Campbell Johnson, originator of the Lay Witness Movement that was sweeping the denomination. John Wesley Church and Danny couldn't believe all of the good things that were happening.

As Dr. Sells had observed, there was considerable spiritual ferment in the church, and it increased over the next several weeks. Sam and Danny continued to interpret the challenge to put God first. The spirit and tenor of the worship services were totally different than in the recent past. Sam was teaching in his Sunday school class. Danny was preaching in the pulpit. The people were hearing something new from their church.

After five Sundays devoted to interpreting the five disciplines, the sixth Sunday was the time for people to respond, and there were twenty-two. Throughout that month spiritual fervor in the church hit an all-time high. Danny tried to ride the wave, but there was so much excitement that it was hard for him to keep up. He had never imagined that his ministry could be like this.

The first group was in March. A second group began in April with similar responses and spiritual energy. In two months, 38 people out of 450 members had practiced the five spiritual disciplines for at least one month and some for two months.

Danny participated, listened, helped Sam lead, prayed like never before, took lots of notes about what was happening, and after two months had a book ready to send to Dr. Sells. It was rough and incomplete, but he met Dr. Sells' deadline. Danny was excited but weary.

He waited and waited, not hearing anything from Dr. Sells. He knew Dr. Sells was targeting July 20 and the big Laity Conference at Lake Junaluska to present the book. Finally Danny gave him a call to say he would be in Atlanta the next week.

Dr. Sells invited Danny to come over and see what his editor had done with the material. They opened the editor's letter together. They were both shocked. The editor was a newspaperman who had taken what Danny wrote and compressed it into two newspaper articles in the third person.

Danny was livid. He thought, "All that time wasted, almost a month!" Trying to hold the wild horses of anger back, he said to Dr. Sells, "If this is what you mean by editing, I think I'm in the wrong place. This is not even interesting! There is no heartbeat to it. There's nothing here that corresponds to what's happening in our church. If this is what you've got in mind, then I'm wasting your time and mine."

Dr. Sells was as disturbed as Danny. He replied with encouragement, "This is not what I had in mind. I'm very disappointed."

"Well, there's a story to be told here, but this doesn't tell it."
Danny said.

"I agree. You continue to work on the story, and we'll get it
out."

It was early in June when they talked in Jim Sells's office.
Danny was in Atlanta to attend Candler School of Theology to
take a TV preaching seminar for two weeks. After talking to Jim,
Danny felt compelled to stay in his room and rewrite the story of
what was happening at John Wesley Church. For all practical
purposes, he dropped out of the course while continuing to
attend classes. He stayed in the dorm and wrote for the better
part of a week.

He went to Dr. G. Ross Freeman, a friend of his on the staff
of the seminary. Danny showed him what he had and told him
what had happened because of the editor. He asked Ross if Jim
Sells could get the book out on time. Ross said, "It looks impossible, but if it can be done, Jim Sells can do it." Ross skimmed the
material. "This is a story that must be told!" He cancelled his
appointments and immediately sat down with Danny so they
could get to work. They wrote the table of contents in an hour or
so, the same table of contents that appeared in the first version of
the book, *A Life That Really Matters*.

Ross was highly skilled in communication, writing, and
editing. Ross and Danny reorganized the structure of the manuscript and began to clearly see the total concept of the book.

With Ross's encouragement and supervision, Danny
continued to give it everything he had. He worked on the manuscript for the better part of the second week. Daily, he turned
additional copy over to Jim in longhand. Jim's secretary typed it.
Jim edited it day and night. It was rushed to the printer, some of
it still in longhand. The book was printed.

The big Laity Conference at Lake Junaluska would start on
July 20. They planned to introduce the book there, because
people were coming from all over the Southeast. About twelve
hundred people were expected. Since Jim Sells was in charge of
that conference, he could say, "Here's a book I want you all to
know about." He was in the position to unveil and feature
Danny's first book, *A Life That Really Matters*.

Danny and Rosalie arrived for the conference the day before, July 19. At ten o'clock that night, they went to the bus station and received the delivery of the book. The next day, it was introduced.

On July 20, 1965, Danny, that country boy from DeFuniak Springs, was asked to introduce Sam Teague, his lay mentor. In that session his book had just been unveiled, and twelve hundred people in attendance sat ready to hear the exciting things God was doing at John Wesley Church. It was a Cinderella kind of experience for Sam and the country boy from DeFuniak Springs.

Sam, a gifted and powerful speaker, took the platform. He shared his experience of despair and frustration with the lack of spiritual progress in his Sunday school class. He spoke of the spine-tingling inspiration that caused him to write the five spiritual disciplines and the rest of the challenge. He invited the audience to return to a faith experience that had been vital and transforming for John Wesley Church.

As Sam was finishing his message, he looked toward the back of the auditorium and saw Joanne Surles entering the auditorium. She was a member of the prayer group at John Wesley, and for days had been insisting to Danny that she was to address the Laity Conference. Both Danny and Sam had thought that was bizarre. The agenda was tight and had been planned for months. Nevertheless, Sam found himself saying, "You know, folks, ladies and gentlemen, one of the members of our prayer group has just walked into the auditorium. She has told us she's supposed to speak to this group."

The audience began to clap and shout, "Yeah, bring her on! Yeah!"

Joanne was ushered to the front. With no training for this sort of thing and "scared to death," she stood up, grabbed that pulpit on both sides and spoke with remarkable power for about twenty minutes. She told them the story of her life, how she used to be, how Christ came into her life, and how her life was now. She was radiant and communicated beautifully.

There was a sense of destiny in the air, that this was a very special time and place, that God was in their midst in some palpable way. Since more program was scheduled, and they were already running behind, Sam stepped in and thanked Joanne for her witness and said, "We've got to stop now and make a transition here. Joanne is going over to the chapel. She'll be there in case any of you want to ask her any questions or talk to her. (She was the same person that had gotten Happy's attention several weeks earlier.)

It was like a light turned on in that Laity Conference, a light of grace. Joanne was escorted to the chapel. Two hundred men and women got up and followed her. The chapel held about two hundred, and it was filled. She continued sharing what was taking place in her life. Before it was over, there was an altar call. People were weeping, coming forward, and praying. She was there with them for almost an hour. When it ended, she walked up to Danny and said it was time for her to go home. He called late that night and got her a plane ticket. She went back to Tallahassee the next morning.

This kind of *kairos* event was happening to a lot of people back at John Wesley Church. And now the whole Southeastern Jurisdiction was impacted. The concept of the Great Experiment caught fire, and the next thing Danny knew, the church was getting calls from all over. Danny remembers, "I see it as a remarkable story, an expression of God's grace. I don't see it as remarkable because it's me, or happened to me. I think God's grace is remarkable. Take a mediocre student, a dried-up preacher who's just getting started, and do something in spite of that. I like the loose translation, 'God works in strange and mischievous ways our blunders to reform.' That's been the story of my life in a sense. That is why I say this is a remarkable expression of grace."

The movement gained considerable momentum through the presentation of the program and materials at Lake Junaluska. The word was out now. People began calling in and writing in for more information.

All of this excitement and extra work began to take its toll on Danny. His thoughts began to turn again to the possibility of getting a new church. He was realizing that the better things are, the more was on his shoulders. He had thirty-eight people giving seventy-six hours a week in ministry service to the church. All the yards had been manicured, all the walls had been painted. There were now curtains in every room. The choir had two more people than they could seat. They had their biggest Vacation Church School that year. All the teachers needed for the school volunteered within fifteen minutes after the announcement was made asking for help. For everything they did they had able bodies saying in essence, "I'll do it, not because it's my duty, but I want to do it because this is the way to live out my faith commitment." Even though it was revolutionary, giving Danny more hope for his ministry, he badly needed some rest, a change of pace. He was already weary from being burned out spiritually, then this intensive wave hit. He felt like he was riding a wild horse. Much of the time he was in over his head and didn't know what he was doing. He had to improvise as he went along.

Nobody in the church knew how to handle the situation, but what was happening felt right and it was obvious that the Spirit was moving. As Danny began reflecting over his recent years, he realized how fortunate he was to have mentors like Sam Teague, Jim Sells, and Ross Freeman. There was also Thomas A. Carruth, whose Christian commitment and devotion to prayer had a formative influence upon Danny over a number of years. Later, there would be Bishop Rueben Job, who mentored Danny as an unofficial spiritual guide for more than a quarter of a century. There was also Father Robert, a Trappist hermit, who taught Danny more about intercessory prayer in less than an hour than he had ever known before or imagined could be known.

Danny could see that his hunch had been right to start a new church. It was needed and had grown well. It was flourishing and had a life and vitality of its own like no other church he had been a part of. He was learning he couldn't coast in taking care of his own spirituality, but that he needed prayer if he wanted to escape the doldrums of spiritual dryness that could come if he was too busy. What he hadn't counted on was fatigue *because the Spirit was moving so dramatically in the life of the congregation.* Previously, when he had experienced spiritual burnout, he thought having a new church would refresh him. Now that this church was new he thought how ironic that new life in the church would produce such fatigue. He didn't expect it to be that way.

CHAPTER SIX

Transition Is Not All Bad

Moving on to a New and Larger World

A deep stirring of spirituality was taking place at John Wesley. But for some reason, instead of this being something to celebrate within the Florida Conference, Danny was told by a couple of colleagues there was a feeling that John Wesley Church needed to be carefully watched. He was told that a "hot spot," an *overly spiritual* church, could go off the deep end and get to be a problem church with a pastor that might be hard to "move." There had been some bad experiences in a few churches when preachers were moved. A friend of Danny's told him that, without realizing it, he had fallen into this category—a preacher that might be hard to move.

With all of this static, with the avalanche of revival that had hit John Wesley Church that he was trying to manage, and facing exhaustion, Danny began to search for some relief. As he reflected on his situation, he considered a particular source of his weariness. Some of it came from the resistance in the church by members of the congregation who were not involved in the Great Experiment and felt threatened by it. Almost overnight there had come a complete turnover of leadership, and this had been a threat to some. People who had official titles but were not fulfilling their responsibilities were left sitting on the sidelines as new people came to life spiritually. There was some resentment about that.

None of this was enough for Danny to have to leave the church. He was also drained in a good sense, drained by all the fervor caused by what was happening.

Danny was offered a church in Orange Park, Florida. So, when he was asked to move, he and Rosalie thought, "It's going to come sometime, if not this year, then next year. It looks like a nice church to go to." So they agreed to move, but it was wrenching to leave John Wesley.

John Wesley Church went through a long season of difficult transition after Danny left. When the founding pastor leaves a church, it makes it doubly challenging for a congregation to adjust to a new pastor. Danny said, "The pastor who followed me had a different philosophy of ministry that was not compatible with the Great Experiment." The emphasis for which the church had become known was placed on the shelf and ignored until the appointment of the third pastor after Danny.

Finally, Tom Farmer was appointed pastor to John Wesley. He had many traits like Danny. After he had been at the church for two or three years, he called Danny on a Fourth of July, early on a Sunday morning. The good news he shared with Danny was this, "Danny, I want to tell you that for the last six or eight years this church has tried to ignore the fact of what happened here in the Great Experiment, and all of that has been rather successfully squelched. But, I'm going to see that that does not continue to happen. I want you to know that today I'm preaching about the challenge of the Great Experiment here at John Wesley. I'm going to call for people to do two things: to honor the birthright of this church and to come forward to put God first in their lives."

The next week he called back. "I want to tell you what happened Sunday. It was one of those services nobody will ever forget. I issued an invitation for people to come forward to be in the new groups. Twenty-two people responded."

Danny almost dropped the phone. Twenty-two was the exact number that came forward on the first Sunday he and Sam had offered the challenge almost ten years earlier. Both Danny and the pastor celebrated together as they talked about what had happened.

Tom said, "As long as I'm here, I can assure you, this church will not forsake its birthright and what it has generated by way of a spiritual movement in the larger Church." Tom continued, "I've been impressed and very embarrassed that a lot of people visit this church and say, 'I just wanted to see the church where it all started.' Visitors come to worship here, and I've been embarrassed that nothing was happening, that the Great Experiment was a dead issue. But that's never going to happen again. This is going to be the church where it happened, and *is still happening*! We're going to claim it, and we're going to honor it."

Tom was there for about eight years. He started many Great Experiment groups and continues to offer the challenge in all of the churches he has served since leaving John Wesley. John Wesley Church has had two or three pastors since Tom. All of them have followed in that tradition. It has honored its heritage in the best sense of that word.

When people ask Danny how the John Wesley Great Experiment is doing in the wider church, he answers, "It's sort of like Coca Cola—it keeps grinding on. After more than thirty-five years it's still popular and widely used. Portions of the materials have been printed in seven or eight languages. That's not because of how the materials were written, but because of how well God answered Sam Teague's fifteen-second prayer so long ago. The simple steps defined by the Great Experiment make it possible for people to put God first in their lives."

But what was Danny doing after he left John Wesley? His appointment was to Orange Park, Florida, in 1966 where he stayed for five years. Orange Park, a bedroom community of Jacksonville, was a so-called promotion and salary-wise, a bigger church. They were experiencing some hard times because the previous pastor was not well emotionally. Just the week before the Morris's arrived at the church, the area experienced a hurricane that made Orange Park's yards look like a shambles. By the time they got there, the people were so glad to have a healthy, enthusiastic person in the pulpit that he was welcomed with open arms.

It was quickly obvious to Danny and Rosalie that these were good people at the Orange Park church. Through no fault of the congregation, the church was simply existing and not much more. As soon as Danny's ministry settled in, enthusiasm began to rise and the Great Experiment was introduced. People began returning to church, coming out of the woodwork to get involved.

Danny put his experience of raising funds for a building project to work, and the congregation put its efforts into building a longed-for fellowship hall. Later, one member donated a very valuable building lot for a parsonage. This was a tremendous breakthrough, because the church had a substandard parsonage. Actually, there were substandard facilities throughout. An old army barracks chapel had been put there when the church was begun thirty years before. The chapel had asbestos siding. The fellowship hall was an old wooden building that had been army surplus as well. Danny and Rosalie were there just long enough to see a beautiful fellowship hall completed, the first phase of a totally new replacement of facilities that would follow. Right after they moved, the new parsonage was built.

The implementation of the Great Experiment had a happy result in Orange Park with no tensions. Danny's weariness completely lifted. The Great Experiment had grown to the extent it had become "The Brave Christian Movement." Danny ran the office of the movement out of the church office. He hired someone to come in and fill orders. He guided this small cottage industry and answered calls relating to the Great Experiment challenge. It was Danny's ministry on the side, but it was also incorporated into the church. Nothing was done undercover, and the church knew the extent of the work and the impact it was having on others across the nation.

It was during Danny's appointment to Orange Park that he was invited to spend a month in the Philippines speaking about the Great Experiment. Frank W. Brown was a church member and close friend of Danny and Rosalie. He gave one thousand dollars on the expenses for the trip. Danny's sphere of influence was expanding overseas. Danny went with missionaries Spotty and Miriam Spottswood. He saw The John Wesley Great Experiment introduced in many churches. It was as powerful in that culture as it had been at home. God answered Sam's brief prayer for *all people*. The materials were translated into two Philippine languages, one by a Wycliffe Bible translator and another by a layperson.

Rosalie wanted to go, but family responsibilities and work demands prevented it. As it turned out, her leadership in the church during that month was a gifted spiritual presence. Her prayer life, enthusiasm, and energy were valued resources of leadership. Upon

Danny's return, the people enjoyed telling him that things went better while he was away. "We want Rosalie to be our pastor!"

Because of the deepening discipleship that took place through the small groups, and other features at Orange Park, Danny felt secure about going to the Philippines for this extended period. His confidence in the congregation proved itself. The church thrived *tremendously* while he was gone, some said better than before. The lay people moved in and took up the slack. Again, Danny had found that laity could be empowered for significant ministry. His focus on the laity increased and became one half of his dual focus on empowering both laity and clergy.

Innovative programs began to pop up in the church. In Orange Park, it had been a long time since much innovation had occurred. One idea that caught on came from the Great Experiment prayer group. They decided one way they could witness would be to put Danny's book, *A Life That Really Matters*, in all the rooms of a new, local Holiday Inn. The Jacksonville Naval Air Station was nearby, and it brought a consistent turnover of visitors to the area. The prayer group bought the books, and wrote in the book's front cover, "Welcome to Orange Park. Orange Park Methodist Church is glad you're in our community. While you're here we hope you have a comfortable stay. Here's a book that's meant a lot to us, and we want you to have a chance to read it while you're resting. If you choose to take it with you, take it with our compliments, and we will replace it." Then, individually, the persons in the prayer group signed their names, indicating they attended the Orange Park Methodist Church.

For three weeks, they placed the books in the Holiday Inn rooms on the night table right beside the Gideon Bible. Since there were about one hundred rooms, they had over one hundred books to place plus some in reserve for replacements. Then the manager called and said that Holiday Inn's corporate office had informed them that only Gideon Bibles could be placed in the rooms. Reluctantly, the group went to collect the books, put them in boxes, and stored them upstairs in the church.

Another idea that took off was the "Youth-a-Go-Go" banquet with a steak dinner, the Howard Hangar Trio brought in from Atlanta, and three vintage Rolls Royces (owned by a friend of the church). A driver and Rolls Royce were offered to any youth who requested that they be picked up and returned with their dates. The banquet became a church-wide and community-wide event. It featured a steak dinner, corsages for the girls, boutonnieres for the guys, and door prizes for a boy and a girl sitting in the right chairs. More than seventy people were served at the banquet, including the youth of the church and all adult workers with youth and others. Regular youth attendance jumped from between four or five to forty-five and held there as additional youth ministries began to occur. The entire project was financed by voluntary contributions from workers and other church members.

It all started when Danny said in a sermon, "We can't expect our youth to be challenged by the gospel while meeting in a substandard room with a light bulb hanging down on the end of a frayed cord, and eating a cold hot dog on a flimsy paper plate." The church rose up and responded with this banquet that made a powerfully different statement to the youth. It caught everyone's attention, and the church followed up with many additional statements—a yearly Fantastic Summer Youth Retreat, and the Back Door Coffee House. There was also the new fellowship hall and new youth classroom facilities. The Back Door was like a Christian night club at the church for the youth of the community. They sat at tables in candlelight where they were served, had live entertainment from youth in the community, and were surrounded by imaginative decorating done by the youth of the church. The only way to get in was through the back door. It was a first-class operation.

On September 19, 1970, the *Florida Times-Union* of Jacksonville carried a story about one of Orange Park's members, Faye L. Davis. She wrote a letter to the youth at their summer church camp, marking the envelope SPECIAL DELIVERY, RETURN RECEIPT REQUESTED, and sending it Certified Mail, Deliver to Addressee only. The addressee was Jesus Christ.

When the letter arrived at the nearby post office, the postmaster called Mary Huntley who was a youth counselor of the church helping to lead the yough retreat. She was called because on the envelope were the words, "Attention, Mrs. Mary Huntley." The postmaster told her that he could not deliver the letter unless someone by the name of Jesus Christ signed for it. At first, they thought the postmaster was joking. After some pleading by Mary and Danny and some others at camp, the postmaster consented to check with his supervisor in Atlanta, because this was no joke. After much discussion between them, he was given permission to deliver the letter to Mary who signed with her own name, but not before the youth were told about the letter and how it was addressed.

Mary and Danny made sure the youth would deal with the question, "Is Jesus Christ among us?" This question prompted intense discussion and soul-searching on the part of everyone. The youth, themselves, concluded that the letter should properly be delivered because "Jesus Christ *is* here among—and within—us."

Danny read the letter to the youth at a night gathering in a darkened, vacant chapel, where the only lights were one candle and a flashlight.

Dear Jesus,

I hope I'm sending this to the right address. Someone said they thought you'd be at camp this week. I have had many things on my mind lately, and I felt the need to tell you about them.

I've been very frustrated for quite some time over the depth of my commitment to you, or the lack of it; and I want to thank you for it. Yes, you heard me Lord, I thank you for all this terrible indecision over my questions and doubts about reality and the Bible.

I thank you because if I weren't frustrated now, I would still be settling for mediocrity in my spiritual life, without seeking to find fulfillment through an intelligent faith in you. So, I am thankful that even though it makes me very uncomfortable, I am just beginning to be honest with you about specific things in my life.

Jesus, at first it was much easier to lie to myself and camouflage my failures, but you have taken that ability away from me. At first, I was a little "put out" with you for doing me that way, but I'm beginning to believe that you have something better in mind than I did, anyway. So, all in all, I'm glad you've done it, even though it's causing me considerable disturbance inside.

I think the main thing you've made clear to me in my observations of people is how frightening it is to see people everywhere who are literally wasting their lives with shallow and materialistic values, and who seem content in their blindness until they lose the fire of youth.

Then they decide to settle down to thinking seriously about their spiritual lives, because they cannot help but know that death isn't too far removed from them. I believe, Lord, that this frightens many people into thinking of you. And I don't want that type of life.

I certainly hope you will keep me from wanting to lead a totally self-centered existence, because I shudder to think of looking back upon my life when I am old, and thinking of all the things I could have done for you. I don't believe I could bear the anguish I would feel.

So, Jesus, after at least four months of frustration and seeking, I'm still seeking. I feel that maybe my commitment has been too shallow or I would have seen your plan for me before now. But Lord, I know you realize that I'm a very stubborn gal. And I do hope you won't just give up on me.

I think, Jesus, if you'll just "hang in there" and keep guiding me a little at a time, that maybe someday I'll be something worthwhile for you. I hope you feel like it's worth a try anyway. I want to want to live for you.

I really believe that no matter what experiences or problems you allow me to have, that you are preparing me for something. Please help me to develop my good, as well as bad, experiences into wisdom and spiritual maturity. I hate to admit it, but I can't do that without you.

Lord, I almost forgot to ask you to be very close to all the campers and counselors at Kulaqua. If it's your will, I hope you'll keep the mosquitoes away, and every inner tube intact. I wish I were with them, but I know you had a reason for it not working out that way.

And most of all help them to find reality in your life and
death, and to see that only through the love you've given us,
can we honestly love each other.
And bring them home safely. *Amen.*

After Danny read the letter, he asked the kids if they thought it
had been missent. There was such a sense of the presence of the living
Christ in their midst that one boy said, "I feel higher now than if I
was on drugs." Because Mrs. Davis expressed her own commitment
as well as her fears and doubts in the letter, it helped the campers
express themselves about their faith experiences. They shared from
very deep levels in the candlelight for a long time that evening.

Danny and Rosalie were invited to India for several weeks to
present the challenge of the Great Experiment. His office helper
went upstairs to get boxes of *A Life That Really Matters* to ship
to India to be there when they arrived, not realizing that some of
the books had been written in. When they opened the boxes of
books in India, and realized that many were written in, there was
some momentary embarrassment for Danny and Rosalie. But
much to their delight, the people were touched that American
Methodists would write their personal witness and sign their
names in a book to be given away. These books became the most
coveted, even though they were identified with the Holiday Inn
and Orange Park. This was an encouragement to the Great
Experiment prayer group back home.

It was during the pastorate at Orange Park that Danny and
Rosalie were introduced to spiritual healing. Their second son,
David, had a physical problem that the doctor couldn't diagnose.
Rosalie, anxious to find help for him, began reading a book *The
Healing Light* by Agnes Sanford. She didn't know how Danny
felt because in those days there was controversy around spiritual
healing. Not wanting Danny to know what she was doing, she
hid the book under her pillow, but Danny was too observant to
let that go on for long.

He got her to open up and let him read the book. That was
his serious introduction to spiritual healing and forthright prayer
for healing. Rosalie and Danny prayed for David over several
weeks and were relieved because of his improvement.

A few weeks later when the opportunity arose to attend a healing service with some visiting leaders, Olga and Ambrose Worrall, they went. The Worralls were so far beyond Rosalie and Danny in the spiritual practice of prayer and healing, it was hard for the Morrises to grasp the concepts they presented. The next night they went to hear the couple speak at a second church across town. There were probably fifty people present. Olga called the ministers present to come forward, saying, "I want you to stand here in the chancel area. We're going to invite the people to come up for prayer. I want you to lay hands on them and pray for them. Ambrose and I will be praying behind you, but we want you to do the praying with the people."

This was a totally new experience for Danny, and though feeling intimidated by it all, he went forward to participate.

When it was over, Olga said, "That was beautiful. There was a time that I looked up, and I saw John Wesley standing behind you." Danny questioned her, "You what?" With moist eyes, almost tears, she said, "John Wesley was here tonight. I saw him. He was walking up and down behind you ministers as you were praying for the people, and he said, 'These are my men. These are my women!' He wasn't here long, but I saw him and heard him say that."

For Danny, this was very unusual, but very moving. He began to open his mind and heart to some of the more surprising work of the Holy Spirit, known for years by some, but new to him. Rosalie was his catalyst, and she continued to urge him to be open to seek God in new ways.

Danny continued leavening his ministry with humor at Orange Park. One night they were having a finance committee meeting. There were seven or eight people present in the office. It had been an easy, positive, and upbeat meeting, and people were about ready to leave. Danny said, "I have something else I need to tell you." He took a long pause for dramatic effect, looked down at a paper on the desk and confessed, "Hope you'll understand what I'm about to tell you. I've gotten a lady in the church pregnant."

One man exclaimed, "Oh God! Oh God! Oh God!"

Everybody just froze. Danny sat there enjoying the discomfort that his intended misunderstanding had caused. Nobody said anything else. Danny sheepishly disclosed, "We're expecting a baby." Louis Huntley jumped up, "*You mean it's Rosalie?*" Delighted to have caught them, Danny leaped out of his chair challenging him, "*Who did you think it would be?*" The people practically fell out of their chairs laughing. It wasn't anything Danny thought up ahead of time, just his natural humor.

The word got around pretty quickly that they were going to have a baby. Five months later while they were attending the Methodist Annual Conference, Rosalie became ill and was put on bed rest. Within less than twenty-four hours after returning home from conference, they lost the baby. When they returned from the hospital they gathered the children to tell them. The children cried. They were assured that their mother was all right and that they would still be moving to the new church in a couple of weeks. This would have been their fourth child. Danny said, "It was tough, but the Orange Park Church gave close, personal support. They were just super!"

The hardest thing was not returning several baby gifts that had already arrived, but that was difficult—especially for Rosalie and Diana. The hardest part was not the move to their new appointment in Hialeah—that was an exciting diversion that might have helped. The hardest thing they faced, as with everyone in this situation, was the weeks and months of grieving over the loss of a child they had already begun to cherish.

They remember several aids that helped them cope with their sense of loss and their hurt: needing to be strong in front of, and because of, the children; periods of silence and prayer, separately and together; and there were tears, intermittent talk, and time. All of these helped and continue to help. Both are surprised that after almost thirty years, there is a tender place in memory and emotion that can still become a quiet fountain of tears. Rosalie said, "That was such a terrible time. We didn't see how we could make it through. We made it because of the prayers of so many who loved us. They held us, lifted us, and carried us."

In a couple of weeks after the miscarriage, they moved to their new appointment, First United Methodist Church in Hialeah, Florida. They found another wonderful church of caring people, and together they went forward.

CHAPTER SEVEN

Am I Worthy?
Learning How to Wait

The ministry at Orange Park Church can be best illustrated by the personal remembrances of one of its members, Merle Jackson. This is her story:

When my husband and I moved to Orange Park, we began attending the Methodist church there, the one where Danny preached. One Sunday Danny announced the beginning of "The Ten Brave Christians Program." He explained that to be a part of it, you had to participate from the beginning. He gave all the requirements. Because Danny was sensitive to my needs and seemed to know just the right thing to say, I really listened.

The next Tuesday I had a dream about my father who had passed away. He was sitting in a seat at our church and beautiful music was playing. The dream stayed with me after I woke up, and I continued to think about it.

As I stepped out on our large back porch, I noticed it felt like a storm was coming. It was hot weather, and you could smell the sweet scent of the grass and the trees. My husband and I sat down on the swing and just enjoyed it.

As we were sitting there, I began to feel something drawing me and remembered what Danny had said on Sunday. I thought something was wrong with me, but I didn't know what it was. I said, "I'm going to sweep off the driveway." Moss from the trees had fallen there. I went out in front and started sweeping. I had on just a little shift and some sandals, and all of a sudden it hit me.

It was twenty minutes after six, and Danny had said that the group for the Ten Brave Christians Program started at six o'clock.

We had a washboard road in those days, and I ran back to Jack who was still on the swing. "Jack, how much do we have coming in each month, and how much is one tenth of that?" He said, "What do you want?" I told him, "I don't want you to ask me any questions." He said that was okay with him. He told me to write a check for whatever I wanted.

I got in the car and did fifty miles an hour down the bumpy road, the three or four blocks and across Highway 17, down to the church. I jumped out of the car and didn't know if the program was in the church or the fellowship hall. I saw a dim light in the church, so I just ran, stumbled over some sidewalk, caught myself before I skinned my knee. I could hear music, it was not loud, but it was everywhere. I couldn't help noticing the beautiful oak trees and the smell was delectable.

I opened the door just enough to slip inside. No one could have seen me. Then I was completely surprised by Danny's booming voice, "Come in Merle Jackson. We're waiting for you." I walked down the aisle, and there on the right was the second seat that was open, and that was the seat where my father was sitting in the dream. The same music was playing.

I didn't have a notebook, so Danny handed me one. "Now, we're going to use this to write what we pray about each day of this month." We would be getting up at 5:30 A.M. to pray. That was one of the spiritual disciplines. For twenty-five years I've prayed and studied like we did then. We also had to make notes in a notebook about anything that we picked up from the scripture lessons each day. The first day's was: "If my people, who are called by my name shall humble themselves and pray, and seek my face, and turn from their wicked ways; then will I hear from heaven, and will forgive their sin, and will heal their land" (2 Chron. 7:14).

On that first morning I wrote a whole page and discussed how I felt about things. It touched me greatly because I had such a horrible life as a child. My mother had died when I was six, and we were in boarding homes where we were mistreated. My dad had to work. He had a printing establishment, and he married again, a woman who also treated us badly. I just was not happy. My brother was in high school, and just before he graduated, he had an accident on Halloween. A man shot him and three other little boys. It blinded him for life, but he became the American director for the Foundation of the Blind for twenty-five years.

We continued with the group meetings every week for a month. Rosalie came to our meetings, and she was like sunshine walking in. I kept doing what I was supposed to do—the studying and the praying. But I didn't get any feeling of comfort for the child that I once was. Then through Danny's teaching, I learned that God is love, and all you do is tell what you've done wrong and ask for forgiveness in the name of Jesus. All I can say is that it turned my life around. It gave my life meaning for the first time.

One night Danny wanted us to come to church for "a Last Supper." In a small room he had set up a long narrow table with fruit of all kinds, the bread that we broke, and a cup. It was like Jesus would have eaten at the Last Supper. After the meal, Danny invited us to offer Jesus something—a gift of some kind. I thought he was out of his head. What was I to bring—money or something? That wouldn't do. After I went home, I sat up 'til midnight asking the Lord what I could give. This poem came to me. It was the first religious poem I ever wrote. Danny changed his sermon that Sunday and read that poem and said my name.

In the poem I talk about walking on the edge of life. It is like a dream I had after my mother died. I was walking around the holes in the ground where they buried people. In the dream my mother was buried alive. In the poem I say what I wanted in life. It's called, "Am I Worthy?":

AM I WORTHY?

What shall I offer you, my Lord,
That is worthy of your name?
My life, so many years, you know
Was not given you to claim.

It was more or less a puzzle
With the pieces all awry—

So often did I pray by rote and
Found no answer to my "why?"
"Seek ye first the Kingdom of God,"
Most surely I knew the key—
"That things be added unto you,"
Is all that it meant to me.

Walking along the edge of life,
There was no reality.
Searching, waiting, dreaming, hoping,
When would life begin for me?

You prodded me often, Father,
'Til the pieces fell in place.
Humbly I thank you from my heart
For your mercy and your grace.

And so unworthily I pray
As a prodigal coming home.
"Forgive my wasted years, dear God,
And number me as thine own."

We all loved Danny's absolute faith in the Lord and his conta-
gious good humor. I never saw him anything but smiles. Whenever
you called him for prayer, you felt like he had a direct line to God.

When he was appointed to another church, I thought I'd
never get over it. But he helped me to see that he was only an
instrument. You can join a church, but you can't join a person.

Shortly after Danny left, my grandson, Jonathan, got a
headache about 6:30 one evening, and his eyes burned. Then he
didn't want the light to shine in his eyes. I took his temperature,
and it was 100 degrees and going up. I called my daughter who
came right away and took him home. I told her to take him to the
emergency room, but she told me, "Mamma, please don't get me
excited now, it's probably just the flu or something like that he
picked up from another child."

After they left, I sat down to think what to do next. I learned
to wait on God in that Ten Brave Christians Program. All of a

sudden the words, "Its spinal meningitis," popped into my mind. I was so alarmed I ran down to Sarah's house and pleaded with her to take Jonathan to the emergency room. I told her what had come to me, but she was angry at my upsetting her, and she wouldn't do it.

The next morning about nine o'clock the phone rang, and it was Sarah. She asked, "Mamma could you and Dad come to the hospital? Bring a robe and some slippers." She started crying and between sobs said, "It was spinal meningitis."

I wondered what to do? I called Danny in Miami. He prayed with me right then on the phone. He just lifted Jon to the Lord, and I felt like God had his hand on that child. At that time my grandchild was unconscious. Rosalie assured me that they would be praying.

At two o'clock early one morning, all of a sudden I had the greatest sense of peace. I sat up in the easy chair there at the hospital by Jon's bedside. Jon sat up and said, "Gammy, where am I?" I said, "You precious doll, we're at the hospital, and you've been very sick." "Well I'm fine now," he replied. The next morning about ten o'clock, Rosalie called me. "Merle," she said, "Jonathan's all right isn't he?" I asked her how she knew. She said that at two o'clock that morning she had a sense of relief. The woman who worked for us, Rosie, said the same thing had happened to her.

CHAPTER EIGHT

Country Heaven
A Round Peg in a Round Hole

Hialeah, a suburb of Miami, was the home for the Hialeah United Methodist Church, a church of about eleven hundred members, while Orange Park had about seven hundred. Again, Danny found himself being "promoted." It was actually another challenge of reviving a plateaued and declining church by focusing on ministry and giving hope. He would be working as the senior pastor with a bilingual congregation, with a Spanish-speaking associate pastor, the Reverend Eleasar Legra.

Dandy Dandurand (now Dandy Lewis) was the church director of Christian education. Her first encounter with Danny was an eye-opener. Dandy offered to show him the way to the hospital and courthouse to get his car tag. As they stood in line for the elevator at the courthouse, Danny asked, "Is this the elevator that fell last week?" Others in the elevator turned pale because anything could happen in Miami. Later at the hospital he asked the same question, "Is this the elevator that fell last week?" He was "one bettered" by a man who said, "Yes, and it fell up instead of down." Dandy saw that his response caught Danny off guard, and he was speechless, something that rarely happened. It was obvious to Dandy that he was going to be a fun guy to be around and unpredictable. She learned that not only was he humorous, but he was also a good boss. He made sure all of his staff had Christmas bonuses at the end of the year, which they had never had before.

For some time Danny had felt a strong desire to maximize the renewal that lay at the heart of the John Wesley Great Experiment. He realized a quiet and small movement was beginning, and it needed to have a chance to be expanded, a chance to blossom. He began to have a sense of urgency about it. He was doing his best to promote it by having an office for it and working out of the church in Hialeah as he had done in Orange Park. He increasingly felt like he had one foot in one stirrup and one foot in another stirrup on a different horse. One horse was the local church he served. The other was the larger parish, the bigger field of church renewal, that he really had his heart in and with which he wanted to do more.

Danny and Rosalie brought enthusiasm to the Hialeah church. They were the youngest parsonage family the church had ever had. Dandy Dandurand was the youth minister and had a wonderful program for youth. She had warned Danny about the tradition the youth had about "papering the new pastor's house." Before they had a chance to do so, Danny put them up to papering Dandy's house.

Spontaneity is a gift he brought to his relationships with people. This was illustrated by his effort some years later in Mt. Juliet to arrange David's marriage.

Danny loves to tell how Susan Clemons came into the lives of the Morris family when she walked into church one morning. He looked toward the back of the sanctuary, saw her walking in with her parents, and asked Rosalie, "Who is that girl with Jody and Luther?"

"That's their daughter, Susan, who is home from school."

His surprising response was, "That's the girl David is going to marry!"

"Oh, you don't even know her. Besides, she is going with someone."

More boldly, "THAT IS THE GIRL DAVID IS GOING TO MARRY!"

Ten months later, Danny told the church full of wedding guests what happened after the worship service that day. "I walked up to Susan and her father who were talking in the narthex and said, 'Luther, it occurs to me that we ought to mate our kids!'"

Luther chuckled and said, "I think you're right."

Susan said, "I think you're right, too!" And they all laughed. (He felt that an *arranged* marriage was in the making.)

He called David later that day who said, "Dad, don't start that again. I'm not interested in meeting someone you've picked out for me."

"David, all I ask is that you just come to our church next Sunday. If you are not interested, I will never say another word to you about her—or any other girl."

"And you won't try to fix me up anymore?"

"I promise."

The Morrises and the Clemonses made sure that Susan and David were present on the following Sunday. David came with two members of his bachelor club who were there to protect him—and check her out. Danny brought Susan and David together after church and introduced them—it was awkward for everyone but him. Since both were shy at the moment, they were a little reticent. Finally, in an effort to be helpful and to move things along, Danny said, "Susan, we are going to the Cooker for lunch, will you join us?"

"I'm sorry. I have to be at work at two o'clock. Thank you for the invitation." In two or three minutes, she joined her parents who were leaving.

David said, "Dad, you are something else! You introduce me to a good looking girl, ask her out for me, and get me turned down before I have a chance to say anything." His bachelor buddies liked what they saw, but they wouldn't let David call her for two weeks—it was against bachelor club rules!

Later, David and Susan said they dated for about a month just for their parents. Then they continued dating for themselves.

Not only was this father full of ideas for David and Susan, but there were other ideas filled with fun for the whole church, and, not occasionally, a surprise.

At Hialeah First, one of his ideas was to help the congregation remember the sermon. The idea was to provide a treasure chest in the narthex on occasional Sundays. It contained enough duplicates of one item for everyone in church to have one. It could be anything from "a cross for your pocket," to a "round tuit," to an appropriate card that related to the sermon, to a rock to illustrate "casting the first stone" (John 8:7).

The church also developed a Fall Festival with games for everyone. One of the favorites was throwing sponges at the preacher. There was also an Easter drama involving over a hundred people. Danny was chosen to play the part of Jesus in the first production that was presented on the final two evenings before they left for a new appointment. (Later, Danny told some friends that he came into the church as Danny and left the church as Jesus.) The Easter drama was so popular that they continued producing it for a number of years.

Their Christmas Eve service, planned by Danny and Dandy, was an inspirational candlelight service. At one point the lights were completely turned off. A picture of Christ was then placed at the altar. Because of the darkness, no one could see it from the congregation. The sanctuary was gradually lit up as members of the congregation brought their candles to place on styrofoam sheets on the chancel railing. The candle lighting service didn't go quite as he had planned. There were so many candles put in place by the slow moving crowd the sheets of styrofoam began to catch on fire. Quick thinking and action by Rosalie and Dandy soon took care of the situation. They continually snuffed out candles that burned down too close to the styrofoam.

The church in Hialeah found it refreshing to have a pastor who lived his faith, really believed it, and didn't put on false fronts. To his spirituality he brought his humor and affirmation of others as humorous, creative, thinking people. It was a reviving combination.

But there were some family challenges. David, the Morris's middle son, had his ten-speed bicycle stolen. It was especially upsetting because he had worked during his summer vacation at his uncle's farm to earn the money for it. The church's insurance company refused to pay to replace the stolen bike because it had not been left in a locked room. Danny took up his son's cause and wrote the insurance company about the loss. After several letters back and forth, David recouped enough money to replace his bike.

Danny and Rosalie's daughter, Diana, remembers Hialeah as "not a great place to be." As a young girl, she found herself receiving unwelcome attention for her blonde hair, a rarity in that neighborhood. She kept hoping a move would soon come.

About this time, Danny went to a denominational meeting in Minneapolis. It had a focus on evangelism, and Danny was making a presentation. Dr. Ira Gallaway, district superintendent of the Houston, Texas District, sat in on Danny's workshop. He liked what he heard and took the Great Experiment back to his district. It made a tremendous and positive impact in several churches. He and Danny got to be good friends, and when he told Danny he was moving to Nashville to head up the Board of Evangelism, he broached the subject of Danny's coming to the board as a staff member.

Almost a year of trying to discern God's will lay ahead. Were Danny and Rosalie being called to leave pastoring for an expanded sphere of influence in the larger church? Or, was this a lark that could end up being an interruption and setback in ministry? After all, he might not be finally accepted for the position. The longing in their hearts pulled them toward Nashville, but they wanted to be sure this was not ego and really was God's will.

Ahead of their discernment, ten-year-old Diana was ready to go. She thought Nashville would be a great place, "country heaven," where she could go without shoes and wear overalls all the time.

Dr. Ira Gallaway and Dr. Ross Whetstone hired Danny to become a staff member of the General Board of Discipleship in Nashville. This was right at the time the Board of Evangelism was changed to the General Board of Discipleship. It would be an opportunity for him to use his gifts and experience in writing, communicating, and imagining new programs. Danny felt having this church-wide opportunity was like he was a bird let out of the cage. It gave him the chance to spend more time in prayer, to think, to collaborate with others in addition to developing more spiritual life programs. He would find, however, that having time to pray doesn't cause you to pray.

In May 1973, they moved to Nashville, Tennessee. The General Board of Discipleship (GBOD) was the program board of the church. Danny became director of small group ministries for the denomination. In his usual coy manner, he jokingly quipped, "I ought to be good with small groups, I've preached to one every Sunday for more than twenty years. I didn't intend it. It just kept working out that way."

His task was to interpret the philosophy and develop strategies for small group ministries in the denomination. Danny did training events, wrote materials, and developed several resources, including:

1. *The Intensive Care Unit*—a small group resource lasting four weeks. One of the pieces of this program was the manual, "How to Be a Caring Person." It usually resulted in helping participants in their desire to be more caring persons and focused on the development of caring ministries in their group and within their church.
2. *How to Tell* a Church* (*recognize)—a self-instructional small group resource. It was an eight-week course that helped a group identify the marks of an authentic church and a counterfeit church. It utilizes humor, pastoral experience, biblical insight about the nature of the church, and broad awareness of the latent potential of local churches. This is probably the most fun small group resource offered by the GBOD.
3. *Discipleship Celebration*—a major program for a local church, putting together the Lay Witness Mission and The John Wesley Great Experiment in a unique and complementary relationship. In a fourteen-month emphasis on discipleship, selected visitors from other churches shared what happened in their lives when Christ came in and changed them. They also talked about what has happened in their lives since becoming disciples. The hosting congregation was called to celebrate discipleship and to emphasize the marks of discipleship in both the congregation and the lives of its members. It continues as a viable program after more than twenty years.
4. *Developing Our Family Covenants*—a four-week resource for a family to use during a family gathering once a week. They would be considering family covenants, what they are, naming the covenants they have, making new covenants, and evaluating how they are doing in living out their family covenants.

Part of Danny's contribution to the culture of small group ministry was advocating short-term groups that people could incorporate into their schedule in a culture that is harassed by time pressures. A person might think, "Well, I've looked at what is being called for in this challenge. It's not unreasonable. The challenge is manageable and of relatively short duration. I think I can do it. I guess I could hold my breath for four weeks if I had to."

For three years Danny wrote for *Interpreter Magazine*, a major Methodist publication that goes to all people in the church with leadership responsibilities. His monthly article focused on evangelism.

As part of his position with the General Board of Discipleship, Danny had to travel. His traveling was a difficult adjustment for the family. He did many field engagements, training people for small group ministry and leadership. For example, he spoke at the Congress on Evangelism in Philadelphia, having the largest workshop there—444 people. With his usual foresightedness, he had asked a colleague from a local church to work with him, and together they led this workshop about small group ministry.

Danny didn't let his traveling interfere with raising the children. David remembers that his dad didn't just say "no" but took time to counsel him when he wanted something the family couldn't afford. His parents' philosophy was, "Help them help themselves." Living in "country heaven," as Diana called Nashville, David decided he had to have a horse. His dad helped him get a job on a farm so he could save his money. David did buy that horse. Eventually he sold it, got another job, and saved money for his first car. David said, "This was the way they always came alongside us and encouraged us to set and reach our goals. This strategy for achievement worked at home, and it worked in the church."

After three years in the evangelism section, his longtime friend from seminary days, Maxie Dunnam, invited Danny to join the staff of the Upper Room, where he would organize the Program Department and become the director. The Program Department centered on almost anything that was new and beyond the publishing efforts. The *Upper Room* is a widely known devotional magazine, and also a publishing and program unit of the General Board of Discipleship. Its focus is on prayer and the Christian spiritual life. Maxie was the world editor of the *Upper Room*. (Currently, it is referred to as Upper Room Ministries.)

Maxie noticed a unique gift that Danny brought—the ability to take the ordinary experiences of life and see the work of the Spirit, to see all of life integrated with the spiritual dimension. Danny could make spirituality relevant to daily living. Putting his finger on the key to Danny's effectiveness, Maxie said, "He could make it relevant because he was a growing person. His creative ability was remarkable, and he could channel it into the designing of resources to help others."

Maxie knew Danny was a gifted and unusual communicator, able to put profound truth in very practical, usable, understandable terminology. He was able to use images and metaphors in a way that made words come alive in the heart of either a listener or a reader.

Maxie knew Danny's deep, intimate life of prayer and knew he and Rosalie had a nourishing prayer life together. He valued this facet of Danny's life, because he had seen him face discouragement and the challenge of trying to get across a new idea to people who couldn't easily grasp a new concept. Danny would turn to God in prayer and find the strength to overcome. Maxie knew he sought guidance from God, to know God's will. Maxie waited for Danny to take more than a year to enter into genuine waiting, discerning God's will about the invitation to join the Upper Room Staff. He was refusing to run ahead of guidance, until he was confident that accepting Maxie's invitation was what the Lord wanted him to do.

His sense of humor was well known to Maxie. He especially appreciated Danny's ability to take himself lightly, to laugh with others, not at others. He also learned about Rosalie's "mystical" intuitions when she usually was right. Danny's daughter, Diana, tells this story.

When Maxie and Danny lived a few blocks from each other, they liked to buy things together, like a lawnmower, a rototiller, tools, etc. Along with all of their children, they helped each other build separate horse barns. At one time they were heavy into horses. Danny and Maxie came home from looking over a thoroughbred, fourteen years old for only $150. Rosalie was preparing supper. The more the two men and the children talked about the horse, the more excited they became (and the more nervous Rosalie became). She kept sounding a repetitive "No!" as a decision seemed to draw nearer and nearer. In her nervous self-defense, she cooked up two loaves of bread into grilled cheese sandwiches. Diana said they ate well that night. By the time Maxie and Danny got around to buying that horse, it had been sold. In a barrel race at a local horse club some weeks later, they watched their favorite thoroughbred run through the barrels and right on through the fence. The horse had a hard mouth, and couldn't be stopped by bit and bridle. Maxie and Danny didn't know that about the horse. Rosalie just turned to them and gave them "that look" but didn't say a word.

Above and beyond all of his obvious qualifications, Maxie prized Danny's total commitment to Christ and to ministry. He knew he practiced what he preached, that scripture was the primary shaping spiritual resource for him. As a family man, Maxie knew Danny could be very, very focused when he went about a task, yet turn it off completely and play with his kids when he went home. He knew this because they were great friends whose kids played together.

After a year of prayer and discernment, Danny accepted the invitation to join the staff of the Upper Room. Feeling his calling included prayer, but went further than that, he chose the title Director of Developing Ministries. He did this because he had the sense that there needed to be a number of new resources developed over a period of time. He was correct.

As Director of Developing Ministries, which meant anything new that Danny and his eventual staff of sixteen persons was working on, he stayed on the cutting edge. All of the programs and learning resources they developed were on prayer and empowering churches, laity, and clergy. These opportunities gave him a tremendous sense of freedom and energy to create. Revealing his leadership style as design-developer, his plan was to create something and hand it off for someone else to manage. He uses the words "lateraling things off" to others, a good football concept gained from his high school days. God's providence makes use of all our experiences.

For example, Danny brought the Cursillo movement, started by the Roman Catholic Church, into the United Methodist Church via the Upper Room. He and Maxie brought in Bob Wood to develop a Methodist expression of Cursillo. When the name caused legal ramifications, they changed from Cursillo to Walk to Emmaus. This pattern of teamwork started in the Great Experiment days when he was calling forth and training laity to get on the firing line, to be where the action was. In those early days, he would continue as the administrator and trainer, but the laity would run things.

In the Upper Room Prayer Ministry more than ten thousand calls a month come to the Prayer Center. Danny wrote a helpful booklet, *Any Miracle God Wants to Give*. In it he shared his experience of prayer at the time of the death of his father, learning to pray over his sermons, prayer as a spiritual discipline in the Great Experiment, and healing miracles he had witnessed. He wrote, "It is better to pray the right way than the wrong way. It is better to pray the wrong way than not to pray at all. It is always right to pray, even if you do it the wrong way!"

In his booklet on prayer, he expressed what he had learned from Dr. J. C. McPheeters about five miracles of healing:

1. *The miracle of the instant cure.* These are miracles of instant healing for physical needs. The founder of the Episcopal Healing Order of St. Luke said he witnessed thirty-seven instant healings over his some fifty years of experience.
2. *The miracle of God's undertaking.* These are healings brought about by the body itself or through the ministrations of doctors and nurses. Many have felt it a miracle to have a cancer diagnosed and removed with no after effects.
3. *The miracle of God's guidance to a remedy.* These are miracles where healing occurs when an unusual insight as to a remedy is received and applied.

4. *The miracle of the sufficiency of God's grace.* These are miracles of people living victoriously, whole in soul, but afflicted in body.
5. *The miracle of the triumphant crossing.* These are the miracles of dying in Christ, knowing that on the other side there is relief from pain and deformity, but even better, fellowship with Christ and those who are waiting for us.

Apart from the program resources mentioned earlier, Danny developed the Upper Room Prayer Center. He originated the Academy for Spiritual Formation, the Five Day Academy, and along with Maxie Dunnam, the Adventure of Living Prayer, gave emphasis to Prayerful Discernment, and called forth the Discernment Network of representatives from more than six hundred churches. Since its beginning in 1965, he has administered the Brave Christian Movement, and continues to do so after retirement.

❊ ❊ ❊

Soon after the family arrived in Nashville, Danny experienced a sensation in his chest, a sensation like a bubbling, a gurgling. On his way to work, he went by to see a doctor who bluntly told him, "You're about to have a heart attack." Danny was startled. The doctor told him to go to Baptist Hospital in two weeks and have a treadmill test. Danny asked, "If I have a heart attack in the next two weeks, does it count?" That was a tough two-week period. Every time a siren went off near him or a door slammed, he instantly thought "This could be *it*!"

Here he faced quite a crisis. He had just launched out on a new ministerial career and was hit with the news that he could die, and quite soon, too. Remembering the booklet he had just written, he thought, "What I need is a miracle!"

Because the family always shared their struggles, Danny and Rosalie sat down with Alan, David, and Diana and laid out the situation. To Diana, then nine or ten, it seemed ominous, seeing how afraid her father was. But to bolster the children's and their own faith that all would be well and to get their minds on something else, they took their boat out for some fun. Alan mischievously steered the boat so it would take on a huge wave. The wave came over the bow, startling and drenching Rosalie and Danny where they sat. Diana cried out, "Dad, are you gonna die? Are you gonna die?" Everyone was trying to be positive, but under the surface, that made the tension higher. Not as fragile as she feared, her dad simply sputtered through the spray and gasped for air. Alan started the laughter and soon, everyone had joined in—except Danny. He didn't think it was funny.

One night as he was unable to sleep, he began to rethink the miracles he had written about. *The miracle of the instant cure*—he would take an instant cure immediately, "God, give me one of those." *The miracle of God's guidance to a remedy*—he was willing to go anywhere, do anything! *The miracle of God's undertaking*, through the natural process of healing. He was willing to wait on the outcome, to have patience. *The miracle of the sufficiency of God's grace*—he said, "God if it's your will that I not be a whole person, help me to be half a person in your name. Help me to be faithful. Give me the grace to be whatever I am to be."

Then he came to the last one, *the miracle of the triumphant crossing*. He discovered he couldn't pray it! He tried, but he couldn't get the words out. He and Rosalie had three children by then, he was only forty years old, here was the new job, new career, new opportunity for ministry. He couldn't imagine letting go of this life to take hold of the next. He realized he was not ready to die, not prepared to die. Even in this storm of emotions, he was chagrined by that, pained by it. He couldn't be glad about having a *triumphant crossing*—right now. The timing seemed so awkward.

In a dream later that night, he had the sense of being up on the side of a mountain on a narrow ledge all alone. It felt like he was standing on a high precipice, his back against a craggy wall. There was no place to turn, no way to escape. And if that wasn't bad enough, the ground in front of him was falling away. In the dream it wouldn't be long before there would be no ledge left, for it would soon be sloughing off beneath him.

Danny realized that in this circumstance everything he had ever believed had also fallen away—scripture, all the teachings about God's love and care, prayer, belief in everlasting life. Everything fell away symbolized by the ground disappearing in front of him and eventually under him. Strong imagery.

At this point he awakened and yelled aloud, "God, the only thing I've got left, absolutely the only thing, is that *I believe in you, God!*" Suddenly, the ground stopped sloughing off. Solid ground: "*I believe in You!* I don't make any promises but that. That's bedrock." In his inner vision, he stood there on the ledge and grew calm with his fear dissipating. When he made his simple but powerfully held declaration of faith in God, he instantly felt something happen. He noticed both sides of his chest "suddenly" equalized, and suddenly they both felt the same. Where there had been a weak, anemic emptiness on his left side, now he experienced the left side of his chest as normal, full, flushed. He actually felt the equalization take place inside his chest.

He looked at the clock—eight minutes before three in the morning. A shift, a physiological shift took place in Danny's body, and he knew a *spiritual* shift had instantaneously taken place also. He was so relieved and exhausted from the struggle, he rolled over and went to sleep and didn't wake up until five hours later.

He had no further concern about a heart attack or dying. In two weeks he went to Baptist Hospital. They put him on a very sophisticated piece of heart testing equipment, attached to a treadmill. He was told they wanted him to keep treading for ten to twelve minutes. After less time than that, the attendant came running in and frantically shut off the machine. All attachments were quickly disconnected, and Danny was told to lie down immediately and remain still. The attendant disappeared for forty-five minutes. Meanwhile Danny and Rosalie were perplexed about what was going on and became increasingly frightened. There was no one around. That period of forty-five minutes felt like three hours. The attendant had simply gone to lunch.

When the attendant returned and read the test, he asked, "Why were you sent here?" Danny explained. He said, "I can't see any sign of a heart problem. Your heart's fine, nothing wrong." To this day, Danny isn't completely sure whether he was misdiagnosed, if there was a cure, or if there was a miracle. He has claimed it as a miracle.

Although it doesn't show up on Danny's resume, David tells us that his father is a great speech coach. Because of his creativity and ability to express himself, he mentored David in a number of speeches and articles. This activity led to David's reputation as an excellent speaker, even in high school. Some of his speech contests and parliamentary procedure contests were video taped and are still viewed by Ag teachers in training at Middle Tennessee State University. He shares this honor with his brother-in-law, Patrick Haines, who was a contemporary. Danny said that Patrick and David went to high school to study and ended up "being studied."

David says, "The qualities I most admire about my dad are his people skills, his ability to just be a celebrity, his ease in front of a group, and the way he communicates with people, not only in the pulpit, but in other ways as well."

CHAPTER NINE ▦

Feeder Pens
Spiritual Nourishment at the
Heart of the Church

For Danny, feeder pens are places and experiences of spiritual nurture in the church. The Academy for Spiritual Formation (see Appendix G) was Danny's next major undertaking. It involved coordinated teamwork among many knowledgeable people. His friend and colleague Maxie Dunnam and Danny through him were impressed with the Ecumenical Institute of Spirituality founded by Douglas Steere and others. They discussed the possibility of some kind of an institute for the Upper Room. (They also discussed a publication supporting spirituality that later became *Weavings.*)

The Academy for Spiritual Formation, sponsored by the Upper Room, took the form of a protestant retreat model, which was strongly influenced by Benedictine monasticism. There are both two-year Academies and five-day Academies. The format includes a rhythm of worship, instruction, small groups, daily Eucharist, prayer, and silence.

The purpose was to develop a core of lay and clergy spiritual leaders who carried back to their churches life-giving spirituality that crossed historical and denominational lines. The Academy grew out of Danny's hope for the church that it be a means for renewal and revitalization.

The first Academy was held at Scarritt College in Nashville, Tennessee, in 1982. Its first participants were drawn from among the subscribers to the *Upper Room* magazine, and other sources. When results were later reviewed, participants remarked about their deepened inner life and their broader vision of the Christian faith. Their spiritual lives were more sensitized, and many of them became renewing factors in their churches, both clergy and laity. For pastors, it was a welcome opportunity for companionship and support without the usual competitive overlays experienced in some denominational meetings.

I myself—Nancy Pfaff—have a personal story to add. My life was dramatically impacted in May of 1995 at an Academy Number Ten meeting at the Mercy Center in Burlingame, California. After eighteen years of severe illness, including Chronic Fatigue Immune Dysfunction Syndrome, I received a miraculous touch of God during one of the healing services at the Academy. At this writing, November 2001, the healing is still apparent. I have started my own ministry of spiritual direction. I never believed that I would be able to minister again, beyond the ministry of prayer that I made my central work during my illness.

Danny's wife, Rosalie, also experienced a healing from sarcoidosis. She thought her life would never be the same as it was before she became ill. Somehow she got the strength to attend an Academy. The Spirit of God touched her, starting a healing that has culminated in no sign of the former illness. Other's lives have been changed in radical ways through participation in the Academy for Spiritual Formation.

In order to best understand the inspiration, philosophy, and experience of the Academy, look in on the following interview:

▦ ▦ ▦

Nancy: Obviously there is a great hunger for this deeper spiritual experience. What prompted you to develop the Academy?

Danny: I remember my dry period when I was doing so many things and not taking intentional time for my inner work. I needed a depth and reality I didn't have. The study of theology had been wonderful in seminary, but it was not enough. Activity was not enough. My level of achievement was not enough. After twenty years in the ministry, I was desperate for authentic Christian spirituality. I felt uneasy because, as a pastor, I had been in a position of being a spiritual leader, and I was not much of a spiritual leader. This caused me to have a good deal of frustration and pain. Instead of a cognitive approach to God, I wanted to experience a personal relationship with God. I was given a three-month study leave in 1977, and I was eager for the focus to be on spirituality.

Nancy: What were you looking for, specifically?

Danny: I had three major questions:

1. *What is an effective practice of intercessory prayer?*
   I discovered this question is bigger than three months, and I am still working on it. Intercessory prayer is very important to me and, of course, I do it every day.
2. *What is the future direction of the Upper Room Covenant Prayer groups?*
   In the Upper Room Prayer Center, we eventually had almost four hundred prayer groups across the country. I wondered where these groups should be in ten years in the practice of intercessory prayer. What is their best gift to the church?
3. *How can we train spiritual directors, persons who are available to walk with another to help them make sense of the spiritual journey in real life situations?*
   I realized that I was not that kind of person, but I knew that such persons were needed in the church, and I am still trying to discover how to train spiritual directors— and to be one.
   Training spiritual directors is not the purpose of the Academy, but we ask participants to be under a spiritual director and to be open to being one if they are asked. We are learning a good bit about it as we experience it for ourselves and value it for the church.

I knew I couldn't answer these three big questions in just three months. They are such major questions, I may be asking them the rest of my life. In three months I hoped to gain an informed ignorance about them. I figured *informed* ignorance was better than my present *ignorant* ignorance.

Nancy: How did you go about studying spirituality?

Danny: I asked a spiritual friend to be my guide. I discovered the theologian John Dunne's dynamic principle of "pass over." It was not the same as Jewish Passover. Dunne referred to "passing over" into someone else's situation (walking in their shoes for a time), then returning to one's own setting. This "passing over" and returning is an enriching experience. It helps us see our situation in our church and in our life differently.

I was eager to pass over into a variety of expressions of spirituality because I felt I needed to kick the slats out of my self-made cage of religious provincialism.

I went, of all places, to a Trappist monastery for three days, and later Rosalie and I went to a Benedictine monastery. I prayed the hours with the Trappists and sensed the strength and the struggle of the young monk and the old hermit. I delighted in their eagerness for the new openness that Second Vatican Council was making possible for Roman Catholics.

Two former Carmelite priests who had married former nuns, yet remained in the church, shared their perspectives with me.

I attended a camp meeting. There was a time in the South (and the North) after the crops were in each year when rural people gathered in a central place for good preaching for two to three weeks at a time. The farmers and their families had been out in the fields pretty much alone, and this was a time for camp meeting, for community, for vacation. There are camp meeting sites all over the country where outstanding preachers are invited to preach. There are classes and community meals. There are family gatherings. I wanted to get in touch with the camp meeting days again. I was delighted to be invited to preach for a week at one of the camps during my study leave.

I also went to a House of Prayer at the Cenacle Retreat Center near Chicago to see how they lived a life of prayer. There, I experienced a vital combination of personal and communal prayer. People go there for three days or eight days or thirty-days for Ignatian silent retreats—times of walking in the footsteps of Jesus' life, companioning with Jesus, if you will.

There are other forms of spirituality I passed over into, such as what I think of as "metro spirituality" at Marble Collegiate Church.

The Upper Room has a journalistic spirituality, giving spiritual guidance to others through media such as books and magazines. I wanted to see what other groups were doing, and I visited

Guidepost Headquarters. While we were there we spent a good bit of time at Norman Vincent Peale's Foundation for Christian Living.

Evangelical spirituality has contributed a great deal with its focus on Bible courses, experiences of God in worship, discovering and using the gifts and fruit of the Spirit, consciousness about one's personal journey, and learning from one another.

During those three fascinating months, I felt I was breaking out of my cocoon, my comfort zone, and stepping into boundless possibilities and expressions of Christian spirituality.

Nancy: So, you had all kinds of ideas, questions, hopes. How did the inspiration for the Academy arise out of it all?

Danny: The Academy was absolutely a gift given by the Spirit. There were many moments of inspiration that came to me and to others who began working on the concept. I was always delighted when a spiritual breakthrough came to any one of us because each inspiration brought its own energy and each had its own ring of truth or sense of rightness. But inspiration was not the only catalyst for moments of insight. Many times I had feelings of frustration, of emptiness, with no way to move forward. I would feel stuck! Then a breakthrough would come.

Nancy: Tell me more about those who worked with you and what you were hoping to accomplish.

Danny: I was not working on the Academy for other people or in order to save the church. I was working on it because my personal, spiritual need was so great, and lots of people were telling me they also needed what I was looking for.

Many persons were networked and grouped in a variety of ways to feather-out the initial plan for the Academy. I called together the Academy Advisory Board of twenty persons. This board was the most formally organized group that worked on the development of the Academy. It was made up of a who's who in spirituality and represented eight denominations. Other than myself, some of those involved were Maxie Dunnam, Bob Wood, Douglas Steere, Morton Kelsey, Ezra Earl Jones, Janice Grana, several bishops, Don Saliers, and a former student of Henri Nouwen's—John Mogabgab, a lay theologian who was working on a Ph.D. in spirituality. As an Academy Advisory Board, we

worked together for four years in preparation to begin the
Academy. I had already worked on it for about a year, so the
Academy was a five-year project. After the Academy was
launched, a smaller Advisory Board was selected.

Nancy: Did you get the answers for your three sabbatical
questions?

Danny: They continued to focus my journey and to point me
toward a startling discovery that was even bigger than the three
questions: *In the church there is an absence of concentrated
emphasis upon growing to maturity in Christ.*

Throughout my lifetime we have had a strong emphasis upon
making a *decision for Christ*—making one's initial commitment
(although it receives less consideration today). Even with all the
improvements in church school curriculum, we still need to recover
ways to call forth maturing spiritual disciples within the church—
for the sake of our children and for the sake of the world!

*We need an Academy for Spiritual Formation for the calling
forth and equipping of spiritual leaders!* This conclusion was very
clear, as sharp in my consciousness as if it were a fully developed
photograph in my hand.

Nancy: From that moment of insight, it took five years to get
to the implementation stage?

Danny: Five years! During that five-year period, two things
were remarkable:

1. I never had a thought that the Academy would not work.
2. I never had a roadblock among all of the hoops I had to
   jump through for approval: the Upper Room under
   Maxie Dunnam's leadership, the General Board of
   Discipleship under Mel Talbert, and later under Ezra Earl
   Jones, bishops, laypersons, clergy persons—all were
   enthusiastic and excited about the plans for the Academy.

Nancy: How were you able to motivate those in leadership to
consider such a new and complex vision?

Danny: In a kind of watershed sermon (for me) at a
Philadelphia renewal conference, I referred to having read
Robinson Crusoe again. He built his fences larger and larger until

the animals on the inside were as wild as the animals on the outside. I saw this as a metaphor for the church. We keep moving the fences—making it easier and easier to become a member by not requiring or expecting anything from those who join, or requiring less and less. Too many people on the inside of the church are indistinguishable from those on the outside. Spiritual feeder pens in the church became a guiding image for the Academy itself and for the Academy's emphasis on calling for small groups of spiritual vitality in the church.

Generally, the people around me readily grasped that picture.

Nancy: Do you advocate changing the fences, the membership requirements?

Danny: No, rather I believe we must *build spiritual feeder pens in the church* where people can gather to be spiritually nourished.

Nancy: I'm not sure I quite understand the concept yet. Just how do you see "spiritual feeder pens"?

Danny: Initially, think of an actual farmer's feeder pen that might be put in a field where cattle are raised. To keep them well fed and to keep the feed from spoiling, the hay is put in a feeder pen in the winter. In the church, feeder pens of spirituality might be any number of things!

One example is the invitation and opportunity for people to explore marks of authentic discipleship. Being an authentic disciple of Jesus is not simply trying harder, but rather, it is having a personal relationship with Jesus Christ. It is experiencing a vivid sense of call and empowerment to do something; something greater than oneself. This has about it a mystical quality or a God-participating quality, where the person has a sense of this *spiritual* dimension operating within one's life.

Another example is to regularly gather with like-minded persons to practice spiritual disciplines such as drawing near to God through prayer, spiritual and biblical reading, taking time apart for reflection, silence and solitude, sharing one's spiritual journey with others, working for justice, and by serving the needs of people in one's area of influence.

A third possibility is a leadership support network of persons who have made deep and life-changing commitments to Christian service, commitments that may go against their own inclinations and may even push them beyond their comfort zone. They feel a necessity to respond to this drawing within them of God's Spirit, a sense of call if you will. In the church, we call this "taking up one's cross." People like that need to be with people like that!

What is frequently involved in any of the above expressions of spirituality *is a dying to self and a rising with Christ* in a new response to God in one's life. There is an inevitable aspect of death followed by resurrection that we experience as Christians—something in us that needs to die in order for something fresh and vital to be born. Then we can be open to something entirely new.

Nancy: This reminds me of your own experience with the Great Experiment. When you had your breakfast with Sam Teague, you felt something die within you, your pride, your insecure security in what you could accomplish, and you saw a larger, more compelling vision for the church in putting God first. Would you agree?

Danny: Certainly. When I realized there might not be even ten members of our congregation who would make a commitment to the Great Experiment, I experienced a personal sense of brokenness out of which came a new conviction that my ministry had to change, to deepen, to open to God in some risky and humbling ways—it was a *season of dying and rising*. It went on for quite a while—and continues.

Nancy: How did you ever present such a new concept so others could grasp it?

Danny: In a presentation I gave at the Upper Room, I said, "Try this idea on for size." Then I described the Academy as it was taking shape in my mind.

I asked, "Are you willing to spend five days every three months for two years in a retreat and learning experience? Don't worry about the kids, your job, or the money. Getting the money will be the easy part. Your question, should you wish to claim it as your own is, 'Is spiritual vitality in me and at the heart of the church that important to me?' You can make the question even more personal: 'Will I be open to an enriching experience that will enhance the growth of my body, my mind, and my spirit?'

"The agenda of the Academy will be comprised of biblical content, reading, interaction, spiritual experimentation such as prayer for healing, nutrition, and physical fitness. We will utilize tested tools of spiritual journaling, Christian autobiography, and the contribution that psychology can make to spiritual maturity.

"The purpose is not to train counselors who can hang up a shingle and go into the couch business. Rather, the purpose is to find persons who are called by God and will become equipped by God's spirit for the ministry of spirituality. The Academy will provide the opportunity for persons to pass over into an experience of learning and spiritual growth, returning to the church to be yeast in the dough—leaven in the loaf (Luke 13:21).

"Gifts have been given to all of us. Some of our gifts are being utilized, and some are not. Some are latent, and some have not even been discovered.

"There is a great need for an Academy for Spiritual Formation. It is a dramatic undertaking, and its time has come. The Academy is a call for authentic Christian discipleship in you and me, in the church, and in the world."

I ended my talk with, "We need a bold retreat emphasis that takes seriously the making and training of Christian disciples to call the church to a recovery of vital piety, experiencing the love-relationship with God in the realities of everyday life. We need a core of people who will be spiritual leaven in the loaf at the heart of the church. This is a bold invitation to deep-running people who are the pick of God's choosing!"

Nancy: Help me connect the concept of feeder pens at the heart of the church and the purpose of the Academy for Spiritual Formation.

Danny: If churches are to have spiritual feeder pens within them, the church needs people in the church who are spiritually well fed themselves and can be spiritual feeders of others.

The Academy provides a place and a protected time for those who feel God drawing them to authentic discipleship, a place to experience community with others who are taking seriously their spiritual journey. Those being called forth by the Holy Spirit must be spiritually fed, be godly men and women who are authentic disciples, and be persons who share their experience and knowledge with the participants in the scope of the sixteen Academy courses in Christian spirituality.

Those who come to the Academy feel a desire to move beyond just ordinary "being in church." They are willing to adjust their schedules to attend eight, five-day sessions of the Academy over a two-year period, to expend significant money and time, and to have a willingness to risk being vulnerable among peers.

Nancy: Is the Academy, then, a big spiritual feeder pen where people who are serious about their life as Christians get spiritually nourished, then go back to actually be feeder pens for others in their local church and sphere of influence?

Danny: That's exactly what's happening; both through the two-year Academy, and also through the five-day Academy, which is an introduction to spirituality.

Nancy: You use the words *spiritual journey* and *spirituality* a lot, what exactly are you referring to?

Danny: We're all on a spiritual journey—our life experience of relationship with God. Some are aware of this and some are not. If we are aware of the spiritual dimension of our lives and intentionally bring ourselves into contact with God, we are conscious of being formed, shaped by this encounter. If we are not aware, we probably just want to pay our rent and try to stay out of trouble. Even these persons are formed unconsciously, but they are being spiritually formed nonetheless—negative spiritual formation. Those who are aware of and eager to be deliberately spiritually formed, sense a plan unfolding within their lives, an accountability to God for who they are becoming, and how they will respond to the movement of God's Spirit. They are on a journey somewhere special, they are not just a wandering nomad. They take accountability seriously. They're not stumbling along without focus or purpose. Instead, God is important to them. They are on a well-defined journey that can be seen as they reflect upon the past, in leadings in the present, and in the way they continue to go forward in their experience of God. The Academy gives them a place to be on the journey with others, to experience the corporateness of the journey, and of being a very real member of the body of Christ.

One of the ways of experiencing this corporateness in the Academy is that people participate in a life of common prayer. They unite in prayer that is universally shared with the whole Christian church by the entire Academy community. All participants give themselves to it communally. This is different than personal, private prayer, where as solitary individuals we offer our own prayers to God.

When I spent some time at the St. Meinrad monastery in Indiana, I was surprised that the monks devoted such a little time to personal prayer. I began to see that they were almost always in community prayer. I soon saw that their community *was a prayer*. They prayed in an ancient way, the liturgy of the hours five times a day. I wanted that reality, that communal rhythm, not just a private rhythm of prayer.

Nancy: This seems so counter-cultural for Americans. Have you seen very many take advantage of the Academy?

Danny: Approximately 1,005 persons have completed sixteen, two-year Academies, and about 5,100 have attended approximately one hundred five-day Academies, and the Academy goes on! Through the light, into the fire!

▓ ▓ ▓

And so we see this long-term effort, the development of the Academy for Spiritual Formation, pulling together the spiritual gifts, experience in ministry, talent, and passion of Danny Morris, focusing them in such a way as to help create fire in the midst of the body of Christ, the church. Following the light he was given, he was led to the fire in his ongoing and profound encounter with God. He has discovered a way to share this fire through mentoring others individually and in groups through the Academy. He retired in December of 1998, having put in place a kind of burning bush that continually illumines hearts by *fire that only God can give*.

Danny says with deep affection and genuine appreciation that his associates in ministry, Linda Heist and Jean Poenitske, have rendered selfless service, Christian dedication, and unique administrative skills in helping to manage the process and growth of the Academy for Spiritual Formation as well as the Department of Developing Ministries for a combined total of sixteen years. Each possesses the capacity to keep several balls in the air at one time, and to survive it with grace. Officially, they were listed as secretaries, but because of their high level of spiritual commitment, he thought of them as *associates in ministry*.

The concluding major focus before his retirement, the Spiritual Discernment Network, began in 1994. He had been working with discernment within the Advisory Board of the Academy through consensus decision making, and realized the dynamism it foreshadowed for all Christian bodies. He wrote *Yearning to Know God's Will*, which takes one on a personal and experiential journey in discernment.

He set out to enlist twenty-five churches to form a covenant to work on spiritual discernment in the church, as an alternative to the adversarial system of Robert's Rules of Order. By April of 1998 there were just over seven hundred persons in the network, representing churches and groups.

In the Discernment Network, participants can indicate whether they represent an Inquiring Church or a Teaching Church or an organization. The Inquiring Church is interested in discernment, but has not started to actually work at it. They are looking over the back fence at others who have begun. The Teaching Church has begun to teach about the principles of discernment and decision-making. They are down in the trenches working at it.

Danny and colleagues Dr. Chuck Olsen and Sister Ellen Morseth, B.V.M. coined the term "discernmentarian." This is someone who has become as adept and committed to spiritual discernment principles and practices in the church as a parliamentarian is to majority rule. Schools for Discernmentarians take place several times yearly, and Discernment 101 seminars are regularly scheduled.

The discernment process is about making decisions out of a desire to perceive and do the will of God—to respond to the movement of the Holy Spirit within the group as each individual prays and speaks out of the wisdom gained through prayer and reflection.

To some this may sound idealistic or mystical and therefore unattainable, but when it is actually experienced, one realizes the power and richness of the process. Actually, it is a logical and a heartfelt movement toward finding the most just, loving, and life-giving option possible in decision making. Rather than having the usual majority rule with sensitivity to the minority, each person's input is considered with all ears open to what the Spirit may be saying to the group, with sensitivity to God.

Certain assumptions regarding spiritual discernment are built into the process:

1. We assume that God is self-disclosing and that God yearns for the created world and enters into a covenant relationship with God's people.
2. We assume that God enters into human existence with such vulnerability that people, in discerning the higher purpose of the divine will, are drawn into the vulnerability of God.
3. We assume that the indwelling Holy Spirit is the active and ongoing guide in personal and corporate discernment.
4. We assume that seeking God's will is the ultimate value in our knowledge and experience.
5. We assume the need to participate humbly in a faith community of grace.
6. We assume that people and communities need to patiently persevere in practices related to scripture, prayer, and discernment until God's leading is known.
7. We assume that the willingness to change the heart and to make an appropriate response are preconditions to the gift of discernment.
8. We assume that God uses especially gifted people with skills and insight into the discernment process in the ministry of discernment.
9. We assume that the practice of discernment is ongoing—we discern God's will again and again and again.

These assumptions that are presented and discussed in the workshops offered on discernment prepare the participants to launch out together in decision making from a point of agreement that God's will is highly valued. This practice informs their method of decision making. As all participants respond to the sense of the movement of God within them, a living picture of the divine will begins to form and to take on color, sound, and action.

One can learn a spiritual way to practice loving one another in the decision-making process from Morris's and Olsen's book *Discerning God's Will Together: A Spiritual Practice for the Church* and from various ongoing discernment workshops. This practice of corporate discernment becomes a way of keeping religious groups in touch with the still, small voice of God—a voice that bursts forth with creative vitality. It is anything but business as usual. For those with courage, faith, humility, patience, and perseverance, *light* can be turned into *fire*.

CHAPTER TEN

Always Fall, Reaching
The Only Way to Live

Anew country music song was introduced in the mid-1990s under the title, "Always Fall, Reaching." Remembering his life-threatening auto accident in 1985, Danny named that as a time where he took a fall. It was a fall off of a twenty-five foot cliff in his car, but it was more. Reaching was absolutely necessary.

On that day, Danny was driving home on a back road, after getting a Saturday afternoon haircut, when he was in a head-on collision. It had been raining but stopped after the roads were thoroughly drenched. A young motorist began a slight skid in rounding a curve, and came over into the other lane, hitting Danny's car head on. The car was knocked off the road. It dropped twenty-five feet off a roadside cliff, tore through a four-strand barbed-wire fence, and stopped about seventy-five feet into a semiplowed field. The nearly new car was bent top and bottom and in the middle from side to side. It was totaled out by the insurance company. Danny suffered a severe concussion and a major headache. He and Rosalie initially thought it was no big deal. But, for the next three years until his brain surgery, Danny experienced the recurring effects of a traumatic closed-head injury.

He went through a time of relapse. Because of the extreme symptoms of head trauma, his family worried if he would be all right mentally. He had spells when he couldn't walk upright and when he couldn't think clearly. He was having difficulty with his short-term memory. He might tell you something and five minutes later tell you again. These spells would last anywhere from twenty minutes to several hours.

By early 1988, there was no course left but brain surgery to implant a brain shunt. This surgery would provide drainage and allow his brain to function normally. All of this change prompted a time of major transition in his life and at work. Danny's memory appeared to be somewhat impaired, his humor was diminished, and he sometimes seemed despondent.

There had been incremental adjustments in his work, prompted by the accident. But finally Danny was asked to give up his position of leadership and to take a lower post at the Upper Room. Except for the brain surgery that eventually took place, stepping down was one of the two toughest times in his life.

Danny's chief administrator, Janice Grana, was an able theologian and administrator and had a rare combination of gifts. She told him that Dr. Ezra Earl Jones, the focused, trim, and energetic general secretary of the General Board of Discipleship, of which the Upper Room is a part, wanted to bring in someone else to be the administrator of the Program Section of the Upper Room. She let Danny know she concurred but was sorry to have to be the one to tell him. This was a tough time for him. He had started the Program Section of the Upper Room along with Maxie Dunnam. The staff had grown to about a dozen over the previous sixteen years. His secretary, Linda Heist, indicated that he took the news with grace.

The other tough time was when the Upper Room turned down his book on discernment. He never knew why. The book would later be published by Zondervan, which was a great delight, but did not quite balance the sense of rejection he had felt earlier. Both stepping down and the book had been personal experiences of rejection that were his most painful ever, but they were not the only ones.

These experiences of personal rejection were his darkest night. He was devastated. He felt fully devalued because the rejections felt like an invalidation and repudiation of his ministry, his discernment of God's will, his experience with church renewal, and his spirituality.

Danny has had tough times and hurtful moments including his father's death when he was sixteen; when, in his teens, he learned of his father's divorce; when he was upbraided and embarrassed in his first church board meeting. Rosalie and Danny experienced the death of both parents. Rosalie had a miscarriage. Danny has always struggled with his weight. Both Danny and Rosalie have had several major surgeries. He has had two life-threatening auto accidents with one resulting in the severe closed-head injury and permanent double vision. They also underwent an initial three years of fear and uncertainty because of the head injury. Then came brain surgery and two follow-up surgeries.

These hurts changed the course of Danny's journey of faith. He says:

- They pushed me to go deeper spiritually. My previous experience of faith was not sufficient to meet the challenge of the shattering that came with the rejections. But because of my previous spiritual orientation, I went looking for a more substantial faith and found it.
- They caused me to grow, out of a sense of brokenness. Other dark times had taught me that when I was faced with my own powerlessness and helplessness, and could do nothing but hope in God for deliverance, God would be faithful to guide me, and sometimes carry me, to a new place of insight, wisdom, and empowerment. These rejections resulted in times like that.
- These tough times deepened my prayer life more than anything else had ever done. During the staff adjustment, my prayer was one of stark realism as I passed through three days and nights of great anguish, openly facing the question, "Is it time for me to leave the Upper Room?" Prayer was not ceremony or ritual but praying for keeps. "If it is your will that I resign, then show me that clearly, and help me to know how to do it." I prayed on both sides of the issue, whether to stay or to leave.
- These tough blows steeled my determination to find a way forward when no way seemed to be open. As Rosalie and I prayed, I was not experiencing any consolation about resigning. The more I thought about resigning, the worse I felt, and the more it seemed to be the wrong course to take. I felt increasingly that this was not what I wanted to do or

needed to do. There seemed to be confirmation for staying, although leaving would have been the easy way out in light of the inner pain I had experienced—easier to say, "Well, I'm through with that," or, "I'll show them!" If I left the Upper Room, lots of stress would be relieved. But above all I wanted to do God's will—leaving or staying.

- Praying through the rejections reassured me, because even in my darkest pit, the light never went out. I was uneasy about going to my supervisor and telling her of my leading to remain on the staff and take a lesser position. I knew there could be a desire on the part of my supervisors that I resign, and their response might be, "I'm sorry you made that choice, we didn't want to fire you, but. . . ." God strengthened me to put my heart and my will into the choice to stay.

"God's gift of responding to me in the midst of this heartache proved to me that even when a hurt demands to be remembered, it may still be stripped of bitterness. I didn't feel overwhelmed by all of this, but knew what I needed to do. God gave me the courage to face the worst and to walk all the way through it. What Rosalie and I shared was the will to walk straight through the issue; to find our way through it, rather than to go around it or try to avoid it.

"The gift that this dark night brought is a deep-running sense of God's presence that has not been diminished by circumstances!"

Presence is now Danny's most cherished and personally empowering word.

Life can break or life can make!

One wonders if this profound and life-shaping sense of the gift of *presence* would have come if the story had been different. As hard as the dark night was, he says that it was a minor exchange compared to the gift of God's presence that followed.

As we are informed by Danny's experience, the word *integrity* stands out so strongly. Having the background he had with a praying mother and a loving family was a great help in giving him the firm foundation of inner character and strength to live his convictions in spite of the struggle or cost. Then, marrying a woman who speaks her truth in love to him, relating to children who have grown into the kind of adults that also speak out of their hearts, has established the base of support necessary for him to live congruently with his beliefs.

In the dysfunctional families we see so often today, a child may have to grow up denying his or her inner truth in order to survive. This makes integrity much more difficult. This is a reason why so many leaders never reach their potential. Those who do correct the discrepancy between how they live and what they believe, and receive insight and healing for the past, can eventually achieve the virtue of integrity. In the life of Danny Morris, God has given us a north star for any who face brokenness and choose not to give into it, but to walk through it as he has done and continues to do.

Danny continued to wonder whether those at work were coddling him, just making a place for him out of sentimentality, but really wished he would resign. Rather than guess at it, he had a talk with his administrator, Janice Grana. "I really need to know if there's more that lies behind this change in my position than your desire to lift my administrative load. Is there a latent, hidden, or unspoken desire that I not be here?" He was assured that they did not want him to leave, that the change in administrative responsibility was not a way of gently trying to remove him from the Upper Room staff.

Dr. Jones called Danny into his office and said, "I want to talk to you." His tone was very warm and personal. He told Danny he appreciated the contribution he was making to the Upper Room. He wanted Danny to know that he was a valued employee and that this change did not in any way mean that he wanted him to leave. He said, "If you were to tell me that you are unhappy about this change and feel negatively about it, then I would rescind it. We'd put it back like it was, because that's how much I care for you and believe in the quality of your work."

Although Danny wanted to take him up on putting things back as they had been, he couldn't bring himself to do so. He also felt like just quitting, but he wanted God's will more. He took a week or so to pray about it, trying to imagine not being at the

Upper Room. He sensed nothing but desolation when he thought about leaving. He had no sense of calling to leave.

The fact that Ezra Earl Jones and Janice Grana would take the time to discuss the situation with him, and in such a personal manner, assured him that he was not an embarrassment or that they felt he could not perform his responsibilities if put in the right place.

Stephen Bryant was chosen to lead the Program Section. Danny had brought Stephen, a forever-youthful and very creative person, to the Program Section several years earlier. They were spiritual friends, colleagues who respected each other, and their choice for him to be Danny's successor made the transition easier for both.

The eventual transition from being director of the Upper Room Program Section to being a staff member in the section was a painful time for Danny. He and Rosalie prayed together throughout the transition. It was very difficult to accept the changes.

As they later reflected on that time, they began to discover a pattern in their lives—a dark night of the soul would be followed by a turn in a different direction. Every time they hit bottom, they had the feeling that God was there with them. They sensed God being with them at this difficult time. It was reassuring.

Danny and Rosalie's son, Alan, kept encouraging him to write about his experiences following the accident. "Dad, you've got to allow the pain and healing to bring about new life. With you, writing is a way the Spirit works. The Spirit is pushing you to chronicle your experiences. Through that pain of squarely facing what has happened comes healing and rebirth. Don't write in order to be published. That is not important! Write to allow the Spirit to help you cope and grow. As you cope, your creativity will begin to flow and you will feel better about yourself. Your story is a story that people will understand! As you write about it, you will begin to understand it!"

What Alan observed was that his dad put his life into his writing. He sensed that Danny needed to work through his problems as he wrote, whether the writing was serious or humorous. Alan noticed that when his father was creating, he felt better about himself and about life in general.

His fall had been pretty dramatic—the accident, three years of uncertainty and anxiety, brain surgery, and now a change in the level of his responsibility. Although he hadn't heard the song title back then, he deliberately chose to "fall, reaching," staying open to God's creative, ongoing invitations.

As his health began to improve, he began *reaching* and thinking of new things to develop. He remembered his wonderful association with Jim Wagner, a friend and pastor who was completing his doctor of ministry degree on the healing ministry in the early to mid-seventies. Danny read his dissertation and was struck with its significance. He encouraged Jim to popularize it for publication. Danny introduced the manuscript to the Upper Room Book Department and they published it as *Blessed to Be a Blessing*.

Danny had sensed that Jim's emphasis on the healing ministry was greatly needed by the denomination. He brought Jim onto the Upper Room staff in the Program Department. During the next nine years, Jim Wagner led the way in reestablishing the healing ministry in the United Methodist Church. *Blessed to Be a Blessing* was followed by his development of "The Adventure of Healing and Wholeness," a retreat model that utilized a leader cadre of 150 lay and clergy who were trained by Jim. Jim developed several additional resources on the ministry of healing and succeeded in reintroducing the healing ministry in the United Methodist Church.

Verification of Jim's effectiveness is the incorporation of significant content about the healing ministry in the United Methodist Book of Worship. Much of the content was quoted directly from his book, *Blessed to Be a Blessing*.

Upon reflection, Danny realized that he had a mentoring relationship with Jim that had been highly productive.

He went to Janice Grana and said, "I've got a thought I just want to put before you that's come to me in the midst of all this. I've met a lot of people who have something that they've written or want to write. I think there is a need for a mentor for some of those people. With some encouragement, they could be a source for the generation of resources for the Upper Room. I'd like to have an opportunity to be a mentor to them, not officially, but informally."

He was encouraged to go forward.

His style as mentor was to say to a person, "I understand you're working on a book, [or a program, or a project]. I'm interested in that. I'd love to work with you on it." This would begin an informal mentoring relationship.

After working with ten or twelve people in this way, it became clear that follow-through was a problem. Some people had great ideas, but couldn't get them down in writing. Others simply appeared to lose interest. Some were not willing to reorder their other commitments to accomplish what was envisioned. After one success and a dozen false starts, Danny lost interest in this particular effort at mentoring.

It is something so rare and wonderful to find a willing mentor, and considering the value of such mentoring, it is truly a loss to the church when it is not responded to.

Mentoring is one of the measures of his ministry.

Danny does continue mentoring among colleagues and teams for the academies. In turn, those people are mentoring others. The staff he has developed within the Prayer Center mentors "pray-ers" who pray with people throughout the country.

The freedom from the administrative load has provided him time to add new developing ministries such as a targeted expansion of the Academy model, both in numbers of events and dynamics, and the Discernment Network has also been significant. Danny and his colleague Chuck Olsen have written a book entitled, *Discerning God's Will Together*. In it they coined the word "discernmentarian" as a counterpart to parliamentarian, and have initiated schools for discernmentarians, which provide mentoring through workshop events.

CHAPTER ELEVEN

An Inside Job
Rosalie's Reflections

For an inside look at Danny, let's listen in on Rosalie's impressions of her husband and the ways God works through both of them.

Many people have asked me what it is like to live with Danny. He has never been like my early images of how a preacher ought to be. He hasn't poured over lots of books, or systematically studied Greek or Hebrew scriptures daily, or developed files of "Snappy Sermon Starters" from stacks and stacks of papers or magazines. Instead, he reads scripture and spends lots and lots of time sitting, rocking, looking off into the distance, being quiet, and waiting.

He loves to be with people and is often the life of the party. But over the last fifteen years or so he has increasingly turned to silence. When he studies or writes, he makes few notes, and often they appear to be fragmentary and incomplete. Something is often born that way—a sermon, an idea, an insight, part or all of a vision—is given deep within him. He can never explain how a thing originates or is formed. He just knows when it has. The irony is that he can often be mystical and practical at the same time, and that such an introverted bent resides in such an extroverted person, but that's who he is.

You can't imagine how shocked I was some years ago when I took the Meyers-Briggs test on personality types. I am the most extroverted member of my family of origin. As an R.N., I have had to be assertive and aggressive. As you may have guessed, living with Danny is an invitation to a party, any time, any place. When Alan was just under a year old, we were with some friends in a restaurant in downtown Atlanta at 2:00 A.M. having a ball. Alan was entertaining everyone at our table and several tables around us.

But my Meyers Briggs test indicated that I am a strong introvert! I couldn't believe it. I was really put out, almost angry, because of my test results. Then I cooled down and realized that although I often *act* like an extrovert, I *feel* like an introvert. I get strength from within. I crave solitude and silence. I like being alone. I love it when Danny goes on a trip, and I am home alone to do my thing in my own way. I also love it when he returns, and I am usually ready to catch the ring and go around again. (I have always been thankful that he has a *traveling job*.)

Our two sons, Alan and David, are fun-loving introverts and our daughter, Diana, is a lively extrovert—the same Meyers-Briggs personality type as her father.

When Alan's wife, Beth, was interviewing for a job, one of the interviewers in the group asked, "What is it like to have dinner at the Morris's?" Instead of answering, Beth laughed, and the group laughed. Her response must have been satisfactory because she got the job. If they had pressed her for an answer, Beth could have said that when our combined families (now with nine grandchildren) get together for a meal, it is a loud and fun time. I would add that when we all have dinner at our house, the meal has some characteristics of a safe and well-managed riot: lots of energy and movement, excitement, noise, and in no time, we can ravage a tableful of food! Come to think of it, living with Danny is like a safe and well-managed riot, and I (and surely he) wouldn't have it any other way.

In our early years of marriage, we viewed spiritual breakthrough times as special experiences—perhaps as isolated moments of insight. When something was being birthed in Danny or me, it always brought new floods of energy. As these insightful times increased in frequency and number, they became rather common occurrences, more and more a *way of life* for each of us. We have always thought that God ministered to us in wonderful ways because our need was so great!

I have concluded that a pattern of new ideas coming out of deep contemplation has been Danny's way of prayerful discernment. Over many years he struggled and found it so difficult to know God's will. Early on, he didn't know he was practicing discernment, and he had no historical language to describe it. He just knew that his will was different when impacted by the divine will. That was always an inside job.

The gift of insight and guidance for the John Wesley Great Experiment, given to Sam Teague following a fifteen-second prayer in 1965, was Sam's discernment of God's will and the beginning of Danny's awareness that such things happen.

The Upper Room Living Prayer Center was born from a gift of discernment over a two-day period. Danny said those were two of the greatest days he has ever lived. He didn't realize he was doing discernment. The only thing he knew was that he had a peace about the image of the Prayer Ministry within his being, and it was probably right to implement that image in practical ways. Until he gets that peace, he doesn't act on insights. After many years, he realizes there is much more involved in the experience and process of discernment than he knows, and he is an eager learner.

The Academy for Spiritual Formation, begun in 1982, was a five-year process of discernment for Danny. He and his colleague, Bob Wood, set up a discernment exercise in which Danny tried to communicate the developing Academy plan and clarify it as Bob asked questions. It was like catching moon beams because the more questions Bob asked, the more the Spirit gave Danny answers from that deep center within.

Danny's first introduction to discernment came a few months later in 1983 with the beginning of the Academy. In 1994, he began the Discernment Network *For a New Kind of Church*. Discernment has been so much a part of his spiritual journey, he just had to know more and more about it. Danny was given encouragement from the leadership of the Upper Room to go forward.

His book *Yearning To Know God's Will*, published by Zondervan in 1991, was also a five-year project in discernment. He rewrote it four times, with no publisher in sight. He literally wore out his first computer in the process.

If I could take one snapshot and capture our nearly fifty years together, it would be a picture of hills and valleys, with us living mostly in the high country. There have been some valleys—disappointment, tough times, misunderstandings, heartaches, and losses. Who could ever expect to rear three children in times like these without hills and valleys? And there have been some actual pits—the deaths of our parents, a miscarriage, serious surgery for both of us, a few relationships broken with heartache through death and circumstances, hard transitions, and my broken arm that has gone through two surgeries and will probably never heal. Pits—every one!

When we have stumbled into a valley or fallen into a pit, we've had each other, always. We have tried to talk things through, we've prayed together, and cried together, and laughed together. If it were a valley, we would keep walking. If it were a pit, we would scratch our way up its walls. We knew we didn't belong in the valley or the pit, because we've always remembered our address is in the high country. From the high country, we actually go up to the top of the mountain more than toward the valleys and pits. We hope to be able to live up there someday.

Over the more than forty-seven years of our marriage, we have moved and been moved by our desire to know and do God's will. We are agreed that valuing God's will above everything else is a great way to live.

I told Danny, "You know, we usually do not go far enough in prayerful discernment. We are content to receive even a few crumbs from God's table when an entire loaf is available, one especially *broken* for all of *us*."

When we were first married, I heard that the two shall become one in God's sight. I now realize that part of that mystical union between us includes the powerful fact that together we can know God's will more completely than either of us can know it separately.

CHAPTER TWELVE

Looking through the Curtain
Receiving the Gift of a Special Kind of Seeing

One of the points of focus that has come to Danny and Rosalie in recent years is the unique relationship of their personal spiritual experiences and the spiritual focus of their particular local church. "In the churches, why are we satisfied with less than fire? Why be satisfied with anything less than *the fire that only God can give?*"

To experience spiritual *fire*, this profound spiritual principle still holds: Our part is to *put God first*! This level of commitment is needed as much or more today as when Danny discovered it for himself through the Great Experiment. His secretary from 1977 to 1992, Linda Heist, refers to this emphasis as part of the legacy he leaves, "Danny has developed, or discovered, new ways for people to open their perception to new dimensions of spiritual life." *Spiritual commitment* are two big words for Danny.

At one point in this author's conversations, Danny said a powerful image for him has derived from the curtain of the temple being split from top to bottom (Matt. 27:51). He thinks of his experiences of the phenomenon of *looking through the curtain* as a special kind of seeing which comes all too seldom. Although it has not happened often, those times are memorable, and they indicate that we can expect God to be active and involved in our personal lives and in the lives of others. For him, looking through the curtain, even occasionally and even briefly, has revealed glimpses of God's wondrous reality and Christ's presence. These glimpses have been gifts of grace.

One such time was in 1965 when he discovered for the first time that laity must be empowered and equipped for the ministry of the church for they have gifts and ministries to share. It was a glimpse of a new truth that he has never forgotten. He believes that when any one of us (lay or clergy) chooses to enter into a deeper spiritual life and to be constantly renewed, we can become spiritual persons who are built for distance and for depth.

When Danny committed his life to Christ in service to the church at sixteen, it was a very real moment of sensing God's presence, power, and personal involvement. He would say that this was probably his first experience of looking through the curtain. But if he had not moved on from that *emotional* experience, he would not have survived as a Christian.

During the fifteen years between that conversion experience at sixteen and the beginning of the Great Experiment at John Wesley Church, Danny had very few spiritual glimpses. But in 1965, through the Great Experiment he underwent a monumental shift in spiritual perception. He saw that the God who created the universe was still involved in that creation, and that God could, would, and does pull back the curtain at special moments to reveal dynamic truth touched with glory.

Danny has looked through the pulled-back curtain several times since his ministry at John Wesley. During two days, he was inspired to start the Living Prayer Center by being shown a picture he had never seen before. For a year Maxie Dunnam, world editor of the *Upper Room*, had been asking Danny to join the Upper Room staff as head of the Prayer Department. In *Yearning to Know God's Will*, Danny describes the two most exciting days of his life when he was given the picture of the Living Prayer Center:

▦ ▦ ▦

I had great misgivings about accepting this position and had refused it for a number of months. I did not see myself in that way. Each time I refused the job, Maxie and I would talk about it, and I would be both attracted and repelled by it. I felt consolation and desolation mixed together, and I couldn't sort it out. One day Maxie said he needed my final answer and that he couldn't wait any longer.

I spent a fitful weekend, stuck between both positions. A lot of ego was mixed up in my consideration of that invitation. If you were invited to head up the prayer life movement of an entire denomination, how would you feel?

All weekend I prayed earnestly, but I could not get any clarity in discernment. Finally, it was late Sunday afternoon. I went to our bedroom and shut the door so I would be away from everyone. I told God I wanted an answer: "God, I am tired of being raked across the cutting edge of indecision, and I want to know for sure what I am supposed to do or not do. This straddling the fence is eating me alive. I want to know your will now!"

I was standing at the foot of our king-size bed with my back to it. Suddenly I stretched out my arms to the side and said, "God, give me a sign one way or another." Then I took the "Nestea plunge." I fell back into the middle of the bed as a symbol of total surrender. I wanted desperately to know the will of God. I lay there for a moment with my eyes closed face up on the bed. Suddenly, the room began to spin. I suppose I experienced vertigo. It was frightening! My heart began to race at an alarming rate. Everything in the world was topsy-turvy and moving and spinning.

It didn't take much of that to shake me up. I opened my eyes and was amazed to find everything in place—the dresser, the chair, the room. I lay there for a moment and looked around. But I seemed to be all right. Nothing broken. My heart was still racing, but at least it was working. I wondered whether the same thing might happen again. I closed my eyes, and the intensity of the sensation was greater than before. I was determined to endure it longer, but the vertigo increased so much that I grabbed the bed to keep from falling off, even though I was lying in the middle. When I opened my eyes, everything was back in order.

After I began to breathe normally, I said, "Lord, are you trying to tell me something? Are you giving me a sign?" Suddenly it dawned on me. "If I were to accept this invitation, are you telling me that there would be nothing but confusion and turmoil and chaos? Is that what would result?"

Something inside of me died on the bed that day. I gave it all up—the ego, along with all of the anxiety. "Thank you for lifting this burden," I prayed.

At dinner, I said to Rosalie, "Dear, I've decided that we are not going to the Upper Room."

"Oh? Have some potatoes."

It was all right. It was okay. A decision had been made, and that was good. It was a good decision because even potatoes had become more important. I didn't think another thing about the job offer. The issue was gone, over, settled.

I awoke on Monday morning with vibrant spiritual sensitivity like I had never had before or since—except on the following day. It was marvelous! It was an ecstatic feeling. I felt a surge of strength and power coming into me, flooding my consciousness. I drove to work on cloud nine. While I worked on the usual, natural plane, my mind and my spirit soared. It was an incredibly wonderful, creative day. I didn't tell anyone that I was living in another world as I functioned routinely. I had such a deep sense of joy within me. Insights and conclusions and images were coming into my mind and everything seemed to fit so beautifully.

I went to bed that night with no fear that such a wonderful day would end, and with it, the inspiration that had made it special. Sure enough, when I awoke the next morning, I felt a continuation at the same intensity. All through that Tuesday the same exhilarating thoughts continued. Everything was falling into place. All of my ideas about how a prayer ministry could be shaped had died, gone. Now there was a clean slate, and God was writing upon my imagination what might be. It was beautiful. It was inspired.

On the morning that Maxie said, "I have to have your decision today," I began to describe to him the inspiration that had come to me in that two-day period.

I mentioned several features for a new Living Prayer Center . . . Covenant Prayer Groups across the country . . . the groups would be schooled in prayer . . . they would be linked together by the telephone . . . We would have an Upper Room Prayer Meeting once a month . . . give thirty-minute teaching tapes on prayer to the groups without charge . . . I described the newsletter for Covenant Groups and a philosophy of funding to ensure that we would not ask for money from people who called for prayer.

Maxie said, "I perceive that I have your answer."

The elaboration took perhaps twenty minutes. My reply surprised me almost as much as it surprised him. I had immediately realized that what he said was true. Across those two days of intense spiritual insight about the concept and guidelines for a prayer ministry, I had no thoughts about selling these ideas to Maxie, just the wonder and fascination of sharing them with him. The spiritual gift of those two days had been recognized and confirmed by a spiritual friend—and therein, was a call to ministry for the Upper Room and for me.

▦ ▦ ▦

Rare instances of this phenomenon of looking through the curtain continue. Danny has had the experience of a special glimpse at various times when something would come from deep within—a look through the curtain. At an Academy rare instances of this phenomenon of looking through the curtain continue. At an Academy session in Alabama, the group was invited by the speaker on prayer to imagine accompanying someone to Jesus in prayer. Rosalie quickly came to his mind because she had been in severe, constant pain for months as a result of her broken arm, a nonunion fracture. As he closed his eyes and quieted himself, he had a strong visual image of Jesus, Rosalie, and himself standing together, just looking at each other. He said the image he saw in his imagination was real and powerful. Jesus began to rub Rosalie's arm from her shoulder down to her elbow. As he continued to rub her arm, he put his other hand under her arm and said, "I'm sorry your arm is broken." When Danny looked at Rosalie, big tears were coming down her face. He looked again at Jesus. Tears were coming down *his* face. Jesus just continued rubbing her arm. A word came to Danny's mind, "Presence. What a presence!"

Some three months later, he was invited to enter into another prayer experience at an Academy in Indiana. He wanted to pray for Rosalie whose arm still was not healing. As he began to be open to the Spirit, he again became aware of the same image of Jesus, Rosalie, and himself standing together exactly like before.

Jesus was rubbing her arm, and again tears were streaming down her cheeks. In Danny's spiritual imagination, he simply watched. There wasn't anything he wanted to say or do. Jesus was doing it. Just being there was enough!

Suddenly, he was aware that there were no more tears on the faces of either of them.

When he returned home on the following Saturday night, he told Rosalie all about this prayer time. Then he asked if she felt anything unusual that Thursday afternoon. With quiet joy she said, "I had been crying several times every day, and I haven't cried since Friday morning." He felt that during that Thursday prayer time, he had the wonderful privilege of looking through the curtain.

This looking though the curtain is a mystery and a spiritual gift to everyone who experiences it. For some it comes as a personal sense of presence, for others a profound conviction of truth, and for others deeply held faith beyond the senses. Yet it is essential for each of us to look through the curtain to connect with the Divine when we initially become Christians, and as we grow as Christians. We may not have many such penetrating spiritual experiences, but if we recognize them when they come, we can celebrate the gift they are and the special presence of God who gives them. Otherwise we blunder through them and take credit as if they are our own breakthroughs of insight.

If looking through the curtain is for all of us, and Danny believes it is, *our challenge is to properly position ourselves to do so.* He says, first and foremost, through prayer we can invite God to give us new vision. As we deliberately develop a life of prayer, we place ourselves in conscious contact with the divine.

Second, we can specialize in the spiritual life by setting a regular devotional time for Bible reading, journaling our insights, tracking prayer requests and answers to prayer, offering ourselves in service to the church and community for the love of God and others, and meeting together regularly with others who are like minded.

From John's Gospel, we are also encouraged to be aware of the Holy Spirit in us and with us, revealing Christ's truth to us, comforting us, guiding us, helping us discern God's will. With some attentiveness we will be able to see that the Spirit has been, and continues to be, present and active, drawing aside the veil so that our lives as Christians are not just lived-philosophies, but encounters with the living Christ. And the Spirit is promised to all of us and to our children (Acts 2:39).

One of the things we may also remember here is that a personal relationship with God will not exempt us from the usual hardships of life. Danny and Rosalie have had their share of bumps, bruises, scrapes, and breaks. They cannot tell you what they have escaped by being Christians, only what they have experienced—*presence.*

CHAPTER THIRTEEN

A New Kind of Church
A United Methodist–Benedictine "Monastery"

M ary Ewing Stamps, the first female monk in the history of Methodism, took her vows on February 1, 2001. Today she lives at St. Brigid of Kildare, a Methodist-Benedictine monastery. One of her biggest cheerleaders was Danny Morris. As soon as he became aware of her interest in monasticism, he began calling to encourage her, and to see how she was progressing. He went out of his way to make suggestions and to help financially where possible. Mary likes to say, "He was ferociously dedicated to seeing monasticism come into being through the United Methodist Church." Danny was motivated by Mary's deep earnestness about monastic life and saw her as a "lone swimmer upstream" in her desire. He wanted to help her swim faster and get there sooner. Whenever he thought of her, he called to see how she was getting along on the journey.

What does this commitment to monasticism say about Danny? On the surface Danny, as Director of Developing Ministries with the Upper Room, was charged with following up on a 1984 General Conference directive to investigate starting a monastic community. But this matter ran deeper with him. This was an unusual request and everyone was eager to know if the wind of the Spirit was in the General Conference resolution. Upon receiving the resolution, he could have formed a committee to discuss it, the committee could have decided it wasn't appropriate for the Upper Room, referred it back, and the matter would have ended there. But he really became interested in the possibilities since he had already had a taste of monasticism. More important, as he researched and studied various forms of spirituality, including this ancient way of life, the monastic thing bit him. That is, something deep within had previously stirred him when he met some Benedictine monks at a couple of monasteries while on sabbatical.

Before meeting the Benedictines, Danny visited with another expression of monasticism, the Trappists. Because Trappists are a reformed Order of the Benedictines, the Trappist form of monasticism is more austere. The spirituality of both orders is the same—a Paschal or Easter Spirituality—just as in the church as a whole. Each has its own distinctive ways of seeking silence, solitude, and discipline for the sake of living the Gospel and growing in love, but Trappists practice a more highly structured daily rhythm. They pray the hours, also called the Divine Office, eight times a day. As with the Benedictines, this is the common prayer of the community, and is composed of hymns, readings from scripture in general, rehearsing and meditating upon the wisdom of the church, and praying all 150 Psalms each month in community. The Trappists have more of a desert spirituality than the Benedictines. Danny visited Gethsemani near Louisville, Kentucky, famous in part because Thomas Merton lived his monastic life there. Danny visited with the Trappists for three days.

Guests of the monastery sat in one arm of the abbey church that was built in the shape of a cross. Visitors sat in a high balcony looking down and from a long way off on the monks at prayer. He felt isolated and distant from the proceedings, as if he were watching a staged performance. He looked on in curiosity with questions relentlessly popping up within him. The culture shock was overwhelming. This form of spirituality was all so new. Over the three days he was there Danny attended prayer twenty-three times and never felt moved to pray. This way of praying was totally different from his Methodist upbringing. But he was also overwhelmed with the dawning awareness that monks like these have been praying like this for more than fifteen hundred years. These monks were different from Danny in so many ways. They remain silent "unless talking improves the silence." Danny is a conversationalist, gregarious, a strong extrovert. The monks are comfortable with solitude, while he is relational to the core—a rock-ribbed activist. When the pace of a

```
COKESBURY LAKE 31600
11/22/02  12:39   E      4      9060

Customer Account Record # 0013389473
Charge to Account #

SMALL ITEM PURCHASES
201 8TH AVE SO

NASHVILLE, TN 37203
Telephone # (222) 222-2222

ORDERED BY SMALL ITEM PURCHASES

  1 @   12.95  0664224903  25%$     9.71
                NDSB GOSPEL OF JOHN VL 2
  1 @   12.95  066422489X  25%$     9.71
                NDSB GOSPEL OF JOHN VL 1
  1 @   12.95  0664224873  25%$     9.71
                NDSB GOSPEL OF LUKE
  1 @   12.95  0664224881  25%$     9.71
                NDSB GOSPEL OF MARK
  1 @   12.95  066422492X  25%$     9.71
                NDSB GOSPEL OF MATTHEW V
  1 @   12.95  0664224911  25%$     9.71
                NDSB GOSPEL OF MATTHEW V
  3 @    0.50  X952297     0%$      1.50
                STORE SALE AND MISC TRAN
  1 @    1.00  X952297     0%$      1.00
                STORE SALE AND MISC TRAN
SUBTOTAL                        $   60.76
TAX       @ 6.5000%             $    3.95
TOTAL                           $   64.71
TENDERED Cash    0013389473     $   80.00
CHANGE                          $   15.29

        WELCOME TO LAKE JUNALUSKA!
      THANK YOU FOR SHOPPING WITH US
```

moment slows, he has often been heard to say. "Let's *do something*, even if we have to clean it up!"

While being greeted by the retreat master, Danny listened to his simple directions about room location, prayer times, meal times, etc. Then he asked about the one thing that had not been mentioned, "What is our agenda?"

The monk said, "There is no agenda. That is one reason you have come here." Danny froze inside thinking, "No agenda. What will I do with nothing to do?" He went to his room carrying the weight of his suitcase and the weight of this question.

In this strange and foreign environment, Danny was feeling ill at ease. Even before he got to his room, his cage had already been rattled. He soon realized that he was not particularly excited about their form of prayer. In that setting he became poignantly aware of his nagging reluctance to go regularly to prayer, and even to pray. He read the liturgy and participated fully with everyone in the balcony, except he never felt *moved to pray*. He never got deeper than just reading the words printed on the page. This shallow response came to concern him deeply. He concluded that his heart must be as hard as a rock to be in a place like this and not be moved to pray. Danny talked this over with his spiritual director who had joined him there, but Danny left the monastery with a degree of shame within himself at his lack of response to God in that holy place. If Thomas Merton had been there to advise him, Danny might have been told that these very signs are evidence of not having a call to be a Trappist but don't determine the quality of one's spirituality.

Not willing to give up his research on monasticism, he looked for another group with which to spend some time. Rosalie went with him to visit the Benedictine monks of St. Meinrad Archabbey in southern Indiana in 1983. It is a house of about 130 monks, a university, a seminary, a large retreat house, and the well-known Abbey Press. The grounds were crowned with the beautiful Abbey Church. The Benedictines pray the hours five times a day, rather than the Trappists' eight. At St. Meinrad, for three days he prayed with the monks, lived among them, talked with several of them—including the hermit, who lived separately from the community—and experienced their monastic rhythms. The Benedictines are not drawn to the strict silence of the Trappists, but bring silence into worship and the "Great Silence" at night, which occurs between night prayer and morning prayer. In this community and with this schedule of praying, he began to feel drawn to the prayer times. While sitting in choir with the monks during the five times of daily prayer, something stirred deep within him. He began to actually *pray* the prayers and psalms he was reading. It was a welcome contrast to the way he had felt at Gethsemani where he and the other visitors were isolated from the community of monks. At St. Meinrad Danny and Rosalie sat in choir with the monks. Monks frequently and patiently helped them find their place in the liturgy. Worship was much more participatory at St. Meinrad. Still, Danny had many questions. He wondered why the monks didn't have intercessory prayer? Why didn't they have expository prayer or enter into extemporaneous praying? Why did they not have *sentence* prayers? Why did they read so many psalms? Despite these questions, he continued to feel the movement of the Spirit within him and in these times of prayer. There were no great insights, no brilliant vision or mystical experience. But surprisingly, he felt spiritually at home among these monks. At both monasteries he was impressed with the quietness and the sacred aspects of the two communities, but this was home!

Once he was away from St. Meinrad, Danny realized he missed something, and he wondered what it was. The more he thought about it, the more it came clear to him that the monk's rhythm of prayer—morning, noon, afternoon, evening, and night prayer—touched a rhythm that was already in him, and he didn't know it. He was simply responding to that rhythm. Danny believes this rhythm is in everyone though most of us don't have a way of experiencing it and expressing it.

This visit to St. Meinrad Archabbey was near the middle of his three-month sabbatical focusing on various forms of Christian spirituality. The image of the Academy for Spiritual Formation was already forming in him, and he felt sure this rhythm of prayer should be a primary factor in the structure of the forty days and nights over the two years the Academy participants would be together. This monastic rhythm helps the mind and heart see all of time as sacred and the rhythm acts to unify all of life. John Wesley in his own practice and modeling of the Christian life had a modified monastic rhythm—morning prayer, vespers in the late afternoon, daily communion, and night prayer. It was clear that these movements of prayer should be at the heart of the structure of the Academy.

Danny invited Elise Eslinger of the Section on Worship of the General Board of Discipleship to create an Academy Worship Book that contained hymns, songs, choruses, liturgies for Eucharist, and a modified version of the Daily Office. Prayer and music were at the heart of the Academy, including monastic forms of prayer.

When the General Conference resolution was given to Danny, it felt like a gift. The resolution called for the creation of a "Protestant Monastic Community" within the United Methodist Church. This was clearly not a check-off item that could be handled lightly. It occurred to Danny that he must put together a retreat for key people that would be a discernment group to consider beginning a monastic community in the United Methodist Church. He contacted Dr. Parker Palmer who was once a United Methodist, now Quaker, and then Director of Pendle Hill, a Quaker center for study and contemplation in Wallingford, Pennsylvania. Dr. Palmer was very keenly interested in monasticism and a great technical researcher. Danny made an appointment, and asked him to direct this unique discernment retreat.

As they discussed the matter, a change in the focus was agreed to. The change was from a "Protestant Monastic Community," which was mentioned by the resolution, to an "Ecumenical Monastic Community." They felt it should be open to all— Eastern Orthodox, Roman Catholics, and Protestants. It would not be limited to "United Methodists" but enabled by the United Methodist Church and others.

About twenty people met for four days at St. Benedict's Retreat Center near Madison, Wisconsin. One of the key people in attendance was Father Timothy Kelly, OSB, a Benedictine monk at St. John's Abbey, Collegeville, Minnesota. From then on Father Kelly, who was a favorite faculty person for the Academy, also played a strategic role in helping to begin, shape, and nurture the ecumenical monastic community. Also in attendance were three Catholic Sisters from other religious houses, several Upper Room staff members—including Janice Grana, the world editor of the *Upper Room*—two or three theologians, including Dr. Paul Jones (then a United Methodist, now a Catholic monk), two Catholic Sisters from St. Benedict's Center where the group was meeting, and Abbot Benedict (retired) of St. Gregory's Abbey (Episcopal) in Three Rivers, Michigan. It was quite an ecumenical group.

One of the promising signs was that all the Catholics were very supportive. They knew of other start-ups that had occurred across the years and the centuries. They knew how other communities were started and why some had failed while others succeeded, and they were eager to help.

Another encouraging sign followed the revue of Wesleyan history and the monastic influence on the Class Meetings, the Bands, and the Societies started by the Wesleys. The participants began to realize that Wesley's groups were quasi-monastic communities. The people didn't give up their jobs and move away to a monastery, but they could live in vital relationship with each other according to the disciplines agreed to by the members, and encourage each other in the faith where they were. Wesley practiced his version of a Daily Office. The retreat group began to see that as they studied early Christian spirituality from both a Catholic and a Wesleyan point of view, the closer they came to a meeting of minds. It was an amazing discovery. There was a time when Parker Palmer called for thirty minutes of silence. This was the first for Danny who had never been in a silent meeting like this before. His first response was that five minutes would be long and thirty minutes, well, it would be an eternity. But as he got into it, it passed very rapidly because it was a powerful period of inner quiet and personal discovery. He was not threatened by it like he thought he might be. The spirit of the moment and of the group permeated the silence. The Spirit was also present! It was a deeply moving and invigorating interlude for the community as they sensed God with them and among them.

In the retreat, they discerned that the wind of the Spirit was clearly discernable within the General Conference resolution and recommended that the Upper Room should go forward in the development of an ecumenical monastic community.

Almost everyone in the room was feeling that this was not only an authentic call to the church, but an authentic call to them personally. The retreat group began to discuss how they could implement a monastic emphasis and rhythm in their own lives. How would their families respond if they decided to live in community? What would their children or their spouses say? There was much discussion about changes that would be necessary. It wasn't that people were ready to sell everything and become monks, but they were thinking this was more than a call for other people. They found themselves involved in the call. They began to consider that they could begin some groups where they lived and worked. The groups would study monastic values and would have definite times of prayer together in community. Groups could put an emphasis on more frequent Eucharistic services, at least once a week or more often if possible. When they met in retreat back home they could pray the hours together. So, the retreat group decided to go back and talk to their families about what they experienced on this retreat and what changes might be implemented.

Out of this retreat came the idea of forming a different group to facilitate the calling together of those who might be interested in actually forming a monastic community. Over about a year and a half the new group functioned as a Monastic Design Team that went to various monasteries for learning, for further discernment, and to worship together. The Upper Room put over twenty thousand dollars in the work of the Monastic Design Team. The team visited Cullman, Alabama, where there are monasteries in close proximity for men and for women. They visited Saint John's Abbey at Collegeville, Minnesota, and its sister monastery, Saint Benedict's for women at Saint Joseph, Minnesota. Also, there was a visit to the Trappists at Ava, Missouri, and their related lay communities on the same grounds. All along they were feeling that the General Conference resolution given to the group was tender and significant. They knew they must handle it carefully.

One member of the team was Dr. Paul Jones, a United Methodist seminary professor. He was eager to live in community himself. While he didn't feel called to join this emerging community, he continued living the lifestyle of a hermit while teaching at the seminary. He later surrendered his United Methodist Ordination and became a Catholic priest, and is very supportive of these continuing United Methodist efforts.

A pivotal member of the Monastic Design Team was Fr. Timothy Kelly, OSB from St. John's Abbey. He knew of a United Methodist woman who was preparing for her doctorate in theological studies (with an emphasis in monastic theology) from Emory University in Atlanta. Her name was Mary Stamps.

The Monastic Design Team realized there needed to be a monastic center where persons could make permanent vows to live together in community. The vision included an ecumenical community, open to men and women, and obviously experimental.

There was also a need for less-formal expressions of monasticism. The Monastic Design Team came up with the idea of Dispersed Monastic Communities (DMC). These would be groups studying and experiencing monastic values. In these groups, the average Christian could participate in quasi-monastic life without having to change jobs or leave home. About three or four Dispersed Monastic Communities were formed.

In December of 1988, the Upper Room brought together people who were interested in forming the "parent house" monastic community. Their hope was that some would choose to become members of the permanent monastic center. There were guidelines and suggestions about how to get involved. The group would set their own rules in accordance with some guidelines foreseen by the Monastic Design Team. A group who were present declared that they were ready to commit to form the monastic center. Mary Stamps, a United Methodist clergy woman, was joined by Allen Bryan, a United Methodist pastor, and his wife, Marsha, who was a professional fund-raiser. Don Collins, a clergy member of the Wisconsin Annual Conference, had made the original motion to request General Conference to form a monastic community. He and his wife, Edie, were interested, but chose not to go forward to form community. Katherine Roberts, an Episcopal lay woman and a recent graduate of Candler School of Theology, was the fourth person in the new community.

Also among those present at that meeting were Judy Buckley and Claude Whitehead, United Methodist leaders from Birmingham, Alabama. They returned home enthusiastic about the possibilities of starting a Dispersed Monastic Community.

Gradually a Birmingham DMC emerged that developed their own "rule," a written document that spelled out their guidelines for living as a quasi-monastic community, while dispersed. The guidelines addressed the need for both personal and communal prayer and stipulated that each participant should be an active member of a local church of their particular denomination. When they came together monthly, they had a twenty-minute period of silence. A member of the community would share something about his or her faith journey, after which there might be questions for clarification. Everyone had opportunity to tell about how they had been aware of God in their lives over the previous month. A portion of their rule was read and contemplated. There was a community meal followed by the study of a book that focused on a monastic value. Members took turns presenting a chapter. The meeting that began at 4:30 P.M. ended at 8:00 P.M. with a worship service complete with homily and communion. This DMC continues to meet regularly after more than a dozen years with about twenty to twenty-five present. It is a seed-bed for maturing spirituality. This is the only DMC group to continue.

The four persons who decided they were called to live in community formed the Bread of God Community. They took jobs compatible with living their rule of monastic life so that they could be self-supporting. Fr. Timothy Kelly, OSB, the Benedictine monk from St. John's Abbey, stayed close to the community helping them in the formation process. They lived with a community of Benedictine Sisters. After some months together, the group of four that had committed to form the Monastic Center began to move toward further discernments. Allen and Marsha discerned that they were called to retreat ministry rather than monastic life. Katherine did not finalize her call at that time. Mary did confirm her call to be a United Methodist Monk. The Bread of God Community was then dissolved. They debriefed the experience and had some wonderful sessions about the experiment.

Because the Bread of God Community didn't continue (May
1991–April 1992), this monastic experiment could look like a
failure to those on the outside. No one involved felt that way
about it. It was a powerful experience for all of them in their faith
journey and commitment to God.

Mary then entered into a sojourn with a Benedictine women's
community for two years. She was a United Methodist doctoral
student at the time. After completing the sojourn, she was ready
to see who wanted to journey with her in community.

Danny asked Abbot Timothy—as he had become Abbot of
St. John's Abbey—if the monks of St. John's might be open to
helping the United Methodists start a monastery. Danny was
surprised at his reply, expecting that the official monastery position could have been, "You all leave this alone. We do the
monastic stuff. You do retreats." To his surprise, Abbot Timothy
said that they would seriously consider it and told about a house
on monastery property that they would consider dedicating to
this effort. In the summer of 1998, Brother Benedict Luethner,
OSB, (corporate treasurer and business manager of the abbey and
university) was asked by the Abbey's Senior Council to develop
proposals for use of the two vacant houses on their property. He
approached Mary about writing a proposal for use of one of the
houses as a Methodist-Benedictine Monastery. Mary made the
proposal, and it spent a year going through various committees
before the monastic chapter of St. John's voted on July 13, 1999,
for approval of a rental agreement. While the Saint John's
University Physical Plant crews did most of the actual renovation
work, they did not pay for any of it. Mary raised all of the money
for the work (over eleven thousand dollars). This new community is not financed by any sponsoring organizations. Upper
Room Ministries, St. John's, and St. Ben's are supportive of the
endeavor. St. Benedict's Women's Monastery, three miles from St.
John's Abbey, agreed to join the Brothers of St. John's as sponsors
of the new ecumenical community, St. Brigid of Kildare
Monastery. The Upper Room is also a sponsor, making it a
uniquely ecumenical venture. It seems something of a miracle
now to look back and see that the people in power all along the
way over a period of several years saw the potential of this

venture and were willing to favor it's beginnings. The Upper Room made St. Brigid of Kildare Monastery an Affiliate Organization of the General Board of Discipleship. When the board meets each year, Mary will attend and report as an Affiliate Organization related to the United Methodist Church.

Saint Brigid of Kildare Monastery is in the stream of the on-going ecumenical movement of the church, but it is not an ecumenical monastery. It is a Methodist-Benedictine house.

As a result of Danny's growing experience of silence, his participation in many Academies for Spiritual Formation, and his study of monastic values, his images of God have evolved. He can't really separate the monastic experience from the Academy experience and the discernment work he has done. They are all interwoven in their influence upon him. But one of his images of God in the early days of his spiritual journey was that God's will was pretty rigid. He was not predestinarian, but he pictured God's will somewhat like a concrete cinder block. That is, God's will had a definite shape, description, and location. In his image, his life was like a mature wheat field where God had hidden the divine will like one would drop a cinder block among the wheat. Back then he felt that his task in life was finding that cinder block. He perceived that he was supposed to run at full speed throughout his life in search of God's will for him. If he never found it, that would be a shame, because if he missed it, he would miss everything! As he got close to it, he had to be very careful not to over-run it because he suspected that God's will—like a cinder block—had hard edges to it, and he could be bruised by it if he didn't see it in time and blundered past it.

His image of the divine will has changed immensely. Now, he sees that God's will for him is not rigid. It is alive and dynamic, which means it is not pre-set but remains ever current up to and through each precise moment. God's will for him is being formed and continuously reformed in every instant. He believes that according to his responses to God's movements in his life, and to the responses God then makes to his own responses to God, he can determine God's ever-developing will for him. He sees God's will as being formed and reformed with freshness and with abundant power, in the currency of each present moment.

The big breakthrough in coming to this freer and fuller image
of God's will for him was the realization that Danny—and all of
us—is a *co-creator with God, of God's will for us in every
moment.*

Danny hopes monasticism will invest the Protestant Church
with a fresh, though ancient depth of faith, a faith that is more
ecclesial—the church together, the formed and forming church.
This *new kind of Church* would have a form of spirituality that
is personal to be sure—in the Methodist tradition—but it will
be more than that. Danny says, "We Wesleyans have tended to
focus on the very personal dimensions of our faith journey. I
think the monastic contribution will be to offer a different
interpretation, a fuller interpretation, a personal *and* a
communal spirituality. The basic values of the monastic movement over the centuries have much to contribute to our
consumer throw-away society. These values certainly make a
shattering, but healthy, impact upon every superficial motivation to follow Christ. There could be tremendous benefit in
studying the values of silence in a horrendously noisy world.
Also, there is value in looking at monastic values and the
meaning of poverty and the causes of poverty, in an age of
abject poverty for some and excessive affluence of others. The
place of liturgy in spiritual formation in the life of a person and
spiritual formation in the life of the church is very significant.
'Rootage' is important—the deep roots of our spirituality that
go back to the very beginnings of the church."

Danny says, "As Wesleyans we go back more than 260 years.
But Mr. Wesley didn't start it all in 1738. It actually started with
Jesus! I always counted the period between Wesley and Christ as
those Catholics doing their thing, and I wrote off that period as
having little or no meaning to me—to us! Yet in the midst of
learning about the monastic model by experiencing a little of it, I
have begun to recover my deeper roots, my roots that precede the
Protestant Reformation. One day I realized that St. Anthony of
the Desert way back in 300 A.D. was *my people.*

"I don't see Saint Brigid Monastery becoming classical monasticism. I see it as a new kind of monasticism that is soft around the edges, supple to the touch, pliable and inviting, open to people across faith traditions, and easier to get into and to get out of than classical monasticism.

"St. Brigid of Kildare was a contemporary of St. Benedict in the fifth century. Legend says that Saint Brigid was born as her mother was crossing the threshold of the doorway to the house, making Saint Brigid a 'threshold person who opened doors' and carried the church through them. Obviously, Mary Stamps is a threshold person in 2001, in a different way than Saint Brigid was in 441, but she is a threshold person who is opening a new door and inviting the whole church to walk through it.

"And the three faith communities that support her in forming this new monastic center have crossed the threshold by enabling the birth of a new kind of community."

▦ ▦ ▦

This monastic movement opens for United Methodists and others a way to respond when they feel called to monastic life in our times. In all ages and cultures there have been those called to spend full-time developing their relationship to the Divine and to bringing back to the rest of us what they discover about what it means to be human.

Danny Morris believes that there is untold significance in this simple, little step taken by one person, almost unnoticed, in a quiet and remote location. What does it offer? It can break the church open in many new ways. Danny believes it may be the most significant event with which he has ever been associated.

CHAPTER FOURTEEN

New Every Morning . . .

Danny Morris is a leader who is experiencing what Bobby Clinton, professor of leadership at Fuller Seminary, calls Afterglow. This is the phase in a leader's life when who he or she *is* and what they have *done* are seen as integral to each other. Danny's life and ministry typify this phase because of certain defining characteristics: His influence with individuals and the larger community of Faith continues. Others seek out his wisdom, generously supplemented by his long time soul mate and partner, Rosalie. How rare it is for a leader to reach this stage.

We bring this book to a close with Danny's own words as he reflects on some of his longings looking back over a lifetime of ministry—longings fulfilled and longings he will carry forever.

New every morning is your love, great God of light, and all day long you are working for good in the world. Stir up in us desire to serve you, to live peacefully with our neighbors, and to devote each day to your Son, our Savior, Jesus Christ, the Lord. (from *The Worshipbook: Services and Hymns*, © 1970, 1972 by The Westminster Press. Used by permission.)

"New every morning . . ." are the first words of the prayer that is prayed each morning in the Academy for Spiritual Formation. I look back this morning celebrating just a few of the "new things" that God birthed in me along the way.

131

Something happened that was totally *new* the morning my grandfather took me in his arms as an infant, knelt beside his bed, and dedicated me to God for the ministry.

Something *new* happened each day our mother prayed for Bobby and me, kissed us, and sent us out for a new day.

It was a distinct new morning when Sam Teague prayed, and received a call to *put God first*, and the next morning was *new* for me when he told me about that vision.

These and many others have come to reflect my anticipation of something *new* that is being given by God, just like God comes to us new every morning. I have so many reasons to give thanks for God putting longings in my heart and remaining faithful to nurture and bless them.

Almost forty years ago, as we began to *put God first* in small groups I initially glimpsed the glory of spiritually empowered laity. I devoted myself to helping this gifted vision become a reality. That was then. Today my longing for the fulfillment of this vision seems even more promising. In 2001, the Commission on United Methodist Men selected *The Wesley Experience*, originally called the John Wesley Great Experiment, "Wanted: Ten Brave Christians," as the men's spiritual formation emphasis for that year and beyond. In preparation for that emphasis, Larry Malone of the Men's Commission, Andrew Miller of Providence House Publishers, and I revised the booklet that serves as the daily journal by giving it a face to the future and the new name of *The Wesley Experience*, "Surrendering to the Spirit." I had re-written *A Life That Really Matters* two years earlier just as I retired.

The Wesley Experience is already a low-key, spiritual movement that is occurring in churches all over the country. Rosalie and I fill orders for resources every week. We counsel with pastors, and lay persons, who are excited about presenting the challenge. Even so, we have longed for it to happen here in Mt. Juliet, our own church. This longing is being fulfilled as I write. Just this month, March 2002, our congregation here at Grace United Methodist Church registered thirty-nine participants in four groups to go through *The Wesley Experience*. It was also in March thirty-seven years ago that we held our first group experience of what we then called the *John Wesley Great Experiment*.

What touches me so very deeply is that I am being renewed through the same material and group experience today that Sam and I brought to the church so long ago. At this week's meeting of our group, I gave my homemade definition of a miracle: "Something good and surprising that happens to you or to someone you know, that comes as a gift that you or anyone else didn't cause to happen." When I asked if anyone had experienced a miracle this week, someone said, "I did!" After she told us about her miracle, someone else said, "I had a miracle this week!" Then another miracle, and another; what an exciting meeting! Bob, who is endeavoring to *put* God *first* in his life, told us that he had a low tire and pulled into a place for air, just as a woman pulled in with a low tire. She exclaimed, "I don't even have any money for the air machine." He said he would fill her tire, and he checked for others that might be low. She thanked him for his kindness, and he told us, "As she was backing her car, I blurted out, 'I love you!'" As he told us this he slapped his face and shouted, "Where did that come from? I was shocked! But as she drove away, I realized that even though she was a total stranger, I loved that person. I was filled with love." We agreed that this was a miracle of the "gift of love."

I saw church renewal come to a congregation almost forty years ago at John Wesley Church in Tallahassee. As I see it happening now in Grace Church, the anticipation of our people coming alive spiritually is the talk of the church. We long for the circle to be complete: *for divine love and spiritual power to be incarnated in human form among us as they were incarnated in Jesus Christ, once, and forever!*

I expect miracles to happen when the Holy Spirit is moving in people's lives. I expect lots of miracles, some big and some tiny. I expect prayers to be answered, spiritual break-throughs, conversions, new births through the Spirit, being spiritually anointed, new life. I expect to experience powerful love, to see dry bones walking, and bushes burning. I expect that visions will be received, and witnesses will be given. I long for these to happen. I've seen all of these when a congregation comes alive through the Holy Spirit.

I long for this to happen in every church. We have all been in churches that are spiritually dead and churches that are spiritually alive or coming alive. The contrast is very noticeable. When it's not "business as usual," prayer is vital, Scripture is studied and lived, spiritual disciplines are joyfully practiced, Christ is honored and glorified, and the Holy Spirit is living and active in the church. My longing is being fulfilled in the many churches like this I hear from every week.

I am eager for the joy of the Spirit that is manifested in humor to be experienced as a spiritual gift in the church, and that humor be deliberately cultivated by the church. There are too many congregations that don't laugh much together. There are too many people who almost never laugh. One's church life and one's personal life are not meant to be that way. *Our spirits are meant to laugh*—not all of the time, but more often than they do. Harry Houser of Point Washington U.M.C. humorously observed that "Right after the earth was created, God created humor to keep the thing from blowing apart." I long for the day when the number of times laughter occurred at the Board Meeting will be a *serious* measure of how the meeting went; when something humorous is spoken in the sermon at least every eight minutes; when humor classes will be offered and attended right along with Bible and prayer classes. I want the church to realize that it will be stronger and happier when humor is a regular part of its curriculum and practice.

Ever since I first heard of the concept of "spiritual formation" I have longed for our denomination to take it seriously. All of us have welcomed the birthing of new spiritual formation emphases that invite persons to seriously seek to be formed in the image of Christ.

When I made my Cursillo (that later became the Walk to Emmaus) more than twenty years ago I was bowled over by the depth and winsomeness of the spirituality I experienced. I found integrity in the preparation of lay and clergy persons who rose to the occasion of being spiritual guides and Christian models for me. Immediately, I wanted those gifts for every person in every congregation.

At the closing of my Cursillo I was asked to speak. I spoke boldly of my *leading* to introduce Cursillo into the United Methodist Church through my office at the Upper Room.

Currently, there are 380 communities in the U.S. and twenty-eight other countries. More than a million persons have made their Walk to Emmaus. Thanks to God, it is happening!

It took a deep longing to pull me forward over five years in working on the Academy and never losing my zeal for it. What gave me spiritual and physical energy like I had never known before was the hope that clergy and lay persons: 1) could know the totality and spirit of our Christian tradition and claim it; 2) could experience the power of Christian community; and 3) could appropriate a theology of grace through Jesus Christ. If these could occur, new commitments to Christ and spiritual energy would become "leaven in the loaf."

The results are so vast they cannot be calculated. Personal callings, holistic theology, passion for the gospel and for the church, a depth understanding of the whole of our Judeo-Christian tradition, practical skills in ministry, worship skills and prayer forms that give life, discovering the power of Eucharist, journeying together, being spiritually accountable, and new forms of ministry are not measurable, but they are realities.

More than a thousand participants have completed the two-year Academy and ten thousand have attended five-day Academies. Currently, there are recurring two-year Academies located in each of the five jurisdictions of the United Methodist Church.

Above all, I long to remain open and willing to walk with God wherever that leads. Rosalie and I have been reading our favorite devotional book *God Calling* by A. J. Russell. He collected the writings of two elderly women, who remain anonymous by choosing simply to be called "listeners."

Rosalie just read the following selection on her birthday this month:

Remember my words to my disciples, "This kind cometh not out but by prayer and fasting." Can you tread the way I trod? Can you drink of My cup? "All is well." Say always, "All is well."

Long though the way may seem, there is not one inch too much. I, your Lord, am not only with you on the journey,—I planned, and am planning the journey.

There are joys unspeakable in the way you go. Courage—
courage—courage (pg. 66).

That is were we are now at age sixty-eight.

About eight months ago, when I was praying, I said, "Loving
God, I want to say that I have energy for another project of your
choosing. I'm available if there is something You want me to do!"
That is where I am, and where I want to remain!

Epilogue

I applied to the two-year Academy for Spiritual Formation as a handicapped person—almost an invalid. I was terribly weak from many years of prolonged, painful, chronic illness, and walking with a cane. I did not expect to live very much longer. Gratefully, I was accepted as I was and began attending the Academy.

The first month, January 1995, I hobbled into Mercy Center at Burlingame, California, hoping to gain some strength from the classes and the experience of community. I knew of a spiritual director at the center named Don Bisson, and I wanted to make contact with him. I was having difficulty hanging onto God after so much illness. Don and I met and scheduled a retreat to be held the weekend before the next Academy session in May. He asked me to keep track of my dreams.

I arrived at Mercy Center on Friday before the second session of the Academy on Monday. Don asked me what I wanted to work on, and I responded, "anger." As we worked on my dreams over that weekend, the pain in my marriage surfaced. It was a relief to share that with him. Then came a dream from which I awoke feeling full of energy, and as angry as can be. I literally strode around the Mercy Center grounds as fast as I could without my cane to release the anger. When I talked to Don again, he said that I looked ten years younger.

The shock of being released from pain and weakness was earth shaking to me. I was frightened, ecstatic, vulnerable, and in awe of what God was doing. I was grateful when the Academy rhythms began that Monday. Community and the monastic rhythms held me steady. One evening, at a communion service, I carried a candle to the altar, leading the procession, and feeling this was a very special night for me in some way. The homily that night was about a woman healed after an eighteen-year illness. I counted how many years I'd been ill. It was eighteen. My expectancy rose dramatically.

When I received the bread, the Body of Christ, from one of the participants, a physician, she said, "The Body of Christ for your healing." I echoed in my mind, "for my healing." As I placed the bread onto my tongue, a graced awareness came over me. I moved quickly to my seat and simply stayed with a deep and profound sense of God and my body being one. I was aware of every hair of my eyebrows, every nerve ending within me, every muscle and bone—all of my body was being received and welcomed and valued by Christ. When I lifted my head, I was the only one left in the chapel.

It was at least three months later that I began to realize the healing was complete. This was tremendously exciting, but it came with a high price. I had to face the empty state of my marriage and eventually a divorce after thirty-six years. Today, more than seven years later, I continue in wellness, which has made it possible to complete the book.

I never felt particularly graced like Sam Teague and his inspiration, but I did find myself caught up in Danny's story at several points. Those usually were the points where he got an idea and began to develop it or was in a particularly low or discouraged place and came out of it stronger than ever. These echoed my own life experience and I was reminded of God's working in my own life.

Writing the book was a kind of ongoing thread of putting one word after another in the midst of tremendous life changes for me. I wasn't aware of God's hand on the writing as much as God's hand on me surviving great inner and outer upheaval. The writing was a kind of stabilizing influence, and Danny's expressed appreciation to me was like the sun breaking out from behind a cloud of depression or grief. It couldn't change my circumstances, but it kept me thinking that perhaps I was a person with something to give to God.

I have realized that I started the Academy hoping that I could die loving God. I looked for a mentor and guide and found Danny. I searched my dreams and found that I could walk without a cane. I experienced divine healing and a new, healthy life filled with hope. I have been called to do for others the same that was done for me. I want to provide a place for people to come and find spiritual healing through retreat, spiritual direction, and church renewal.

Initially, all I had in mind was fulfilling an Academy project by choosing to write a thirty-five page summary of leadership principles Danny had learned over his lifetime.

Since I never imagined a book until any number of rewrites and the emerging length of the project, I am completely in awe of how it developed, and how it opens up for others such inspiration and encouragement to live for God. I feel totally graced to be a part of it.

After I finished writing it, Rosalie told me that the book is as much about my spiritual journey as it is about Danny's.

Ponder These. . . .

As you complete the reading of each chapter, consider the following prompts. Have a notebook handy if any one of them invites you to go further in consideration of your faith journey. "Ministry" is interpreted here as belonging to lay and clergy, alike.

Chapter 1

1. Revist your pleasant memories of two or three key people who touched your early life and write about how they helped to shape you for ministry.
2. Revisit a painful event, now harmless in reflection, and write three or four things you learned from it.
3. Where do you see affirmation of your strengths today that are rooted in this early period?

Chapter 2

1. What prompted you to Christian service?
2. What one experience most tested your faith and presented a challenge to you for remaining consistent with your inner convictions?
3. List three or four lessons you learned from that experience that are still profitable today.

Chapter 3

1. Make notes about favorite scriptures or other inspirational writings that are metaphors for your life and ministry.

2. What new invitation is in these for you today?

Chapter 4

1. Describe a time when you had to take a "leap of faith" that required you to reevaluate your values, goals, and ministry.
2. How did you respond to that invitation?
3. If you chose to reject it, would you like to revisit it? If you accepted it, what had to change in your attitudes, beliefs, knowledge, and values?

Chapter 5

1. Make a list of people (and events) who affirm your ministry.
2. Reestablish contact with some of the people whose lives have been touched by your ministry. Talk with them about those days.
3. What encouragement did you receive when talking with these people?

Chapter 6

1. List the four or five key people who have mentored you.
2. Reestablish contact with one or more of your mentors. Share with them how their input and influence helped you.
3. Describe the ideal mentor for you at this time.

Chapter 7

1. Name a major transition period and the most difficult aspect you had to overcome in order to move forward.
2. What was your most helpful learning in your transition?

Chapter 8

1. List some strengths and some weaknesses of your prayer life.

2. Recall any fruit from your ministry that was greater than expected. Note where the fruit can be attributed to faith and the work of God through you (as compared to great effort, etc.).

Chapter 9

1. What kind of ministry opportunity do you desire at this time?
2. Is there an opportunity facing you that will connect you with the necessary role and resources to maximize your potential? If not, can you create such a role or redesign your current role?
3. Is there anything that now blocks you from "paying the price" and "taking the risk?"

Chapter 10

1. Select an experience of brokenness that you are far enough from now to revisit. Reflect upon this question: Is there an invitation that God is extending to you to revisit that place, so you can receive healing from it?
2. What lessons did you learn during that difficult time? Are there any to whom you need to make amends, forgive yourself, and move on?

Chapter 11

1. Ask a relative, close friend, or mentor to meet with you for a session to focus on your strengths.
2. Afterwards, make notes of how their view of you is different than your own.

Chapter 12

1. What experiences have you had in "looking through the curtain?"
2. What insights came from these inspirational moments?

3. Express any longing of your heart for deeper spiritual experiences of God in prayer.

Chapter 13

1. Invite a few people in to celebrate with you the lessons you hope your life teaches and how God has been with you in the shaping process.
2. Write a "My Faith Journey" type article for your church paper on what these lessons are.
3. Express your gratitude to God in prayer for the grace that you have been given.

Chapter 14

1. God puts longings in our hearts that never change with God or with us. What is your longing?
2. After you name your deep longing that pulls you forward and gives you energy, pray about it.
3. When you consider the part that humor plays in your life. and your church, do you feel glad or sad? What will you do as a result of your answer?
4. Is there a "position statement" you have said to God lately, or one you wish to say? Write your thoughts and then pray them.

Family of Rosalie Bankhead Green and Danny Eugene Morris

Families of Origin (*deceased*):
George Venable Green and Gladys (McCraney) Green
      Valdosta, Georgia

Dan Leon Morris and Lucy Lujeania Keggler (Sellars) Morris
      De Funiak Springs, Florida

Siblings:
Rosalie: Elizabeth Westwood Biles
              Valdosta, Georgia
            Gladys Venable Stewart
              Valdosta, Georgia

Danny: Robert de Leon Morris (*deceased*)
              Tallahassee, Florida

Nuclear Family:
Alan and Beth (Kemper), Graeme, Kelsey, and Tanner
      Hendersonville, Tennessee

David and Susan (Clemons), Will, Luke, and Joseph
      Brentwood, Tennessee

Diana (Morris) and Patrick Haines, Ross, Anna Claire, and Carson
      Lebanon, Tennessee

Timeline

NOVEMBER 14, 1933—Birth, "The Bullard Farm" near Glendale, Florida

SPRING 1934—Grandfather dedicates Danny in prayer

JUNE 1944—Tooth broken in diving accident

JUNE 1948—Gives life to Christ at summer youth camp

SEPTEMBER 1949—Father dies

WINTER 1949—Family doctor helps Danny understand his father's death

JANUARY 1950—All-Conference Football Team, guard

SUMMER 1950—Trip with mother; learns of his father's previous marriage and a halfsister

FALL 1951—Leaves home for Florida State University

1952–55—Appointment as student pastor, East Leon Circuit

FALL 1955—Enrolls at Candler School of Theology

1955—Youth minister at Sandy Springs

AUGUST 5, 1956—Marries Rosalie Bankhead Green

1956—Student pastor at Mt. Gilead

JUNE 16, 1957—Alan born; appointment to South Bend

JUNE 1958—Associate Pastor at Trinity, Tallahassee

JUNE 1960—Begins John Wesley Church

MARCH 25, 1960—David born

SEPTEMBER 25, 1961—Diana born

JANUARY 24, 1965—Sam Teague is given inspiration for the Ten Brave Christians Program

FEBRUARY 1965—Dr. Sells asks Danny to write the story of *the Great Experiment*

JULY 1965—*A Life That Really Matters* presented at Laity Conference, Lake Junaluska

JUNE 1966—Appointment to Orange Park, First

JUNE 1971—Appointment to Hialeah, First

APRIL 1973—Moves to Nashville to become Director of Small Group Ministries for the denomination

FALL 1973—Heart attack predicted

1974—Writes *Any Miracle God Wants to Give*

1975—*How to Tell* a Church* is published

WINTER 1975—Develops "Discipleship Celebration;" writes for *The Interpreter Magazine* for three years

1976—Develops "The Intensive Care Unit"

SPRING 1976—Joins the Upper Room Staff as Director of Developing Ministries

1978—While on sabbatical, originates Academy For Spiritual Formation

1982—First Academy

FALL 1984—Asked by General Conference Resolution to investigate starting an ecumenical, monastic community

SPRING 1985—Car accident

SPRING 1988—Brain surgery; released from administrative responsibilities

1991—*Yearning to Know God's Will* is published

FALL 1994—The Spiritual Discernment Network begins

SPRING 1997—Co-author, *Discerning God's Will Together* with Chuck Olsen

JANUARY 1999—Retirement; begins Website

2001—Publishes *Spirits Laughing*; begins writing children's books

NOT RETIRED, BUT REFIRED!

Resources
Written by Danny E. Morris

BOOKS AND BOOKLETS
   A Life That Really Matters
   Spirits Laughing
   Yearning to Know God's Will
   Discerning God's Will Together (co-authored with Chuck Olsen)
   How to Tell* a Church
   Any Miracle God Wants to Give

E-BOOKS FOR THE WEB
   Danny Gene's Big Dog Named Spot
   Specky Baby (co-authored with Rosalie)
   A Survival Manual for Care-Givers of All Kinds

IN PRODUCTION
   Poncho, the Puppy
   My First Trip to Emmaus (An Emmaus Novel)

PROGRAM RESOURCES
   The Academy for Spiritual Formation
   The Five-Day Academy
   The Upper Room Living Prayer Center
   The Intensive Care Unit
   How to Tell* a Church
   Discipleship Celebration
   Developing Our Family Covenants
   The "Pray Where You Are" Prayer Packet
   The Adventure of Living Prayer (co-authored with Maxie Dunnam)
   The "I Care" Bracelet

NOVELTY
   'Round Tuit—"I will put God first in my life when I get around tuit."

WEB SITE ON SPIRITUALITY AND HUMOR
   www.spiritslaughing.com/ (under terms spirituality and humor)
   (rated #1 on America Online, Yahoo, Google, Metacrawler, and
   Dogpile search engines.)

APPENDIX E

Excerpts

From Recent Settings

"Memories are about *tomorrow*, because they help to shape it."

Said tongue in cheek to the first meeting of the Monastic Design Team called together to consider beginning an ecumenical monastic community:
"I have been thinking of monastic vows I would like to suggest. I will list the monastic vow first, followed by the monastic value the vow would implement.

Monastic Vow: Vow of Mediocrity
Monastic Value: Improvement is always possible
Monastic Vow: Vow of Profundity
Monastic Value: Desire to eventually say something worthwhile
Monastic Vow: Vow of Puberty
Monastic Value: Remaining young-at-heart

Perhaps this group can develop better vows for the new community!"
After the laughter, someone spoke for the group, "We would sure like to try!"

From A Life That Really Matters

1. And how many times in these more than two hundred years has the church been called to "return"? To recover the sort of spiritual discipline strong enough to give a man of small physical stature a heart big enough for the whole world? A spiritual discipline that was strong enough to give to the world—to life itself—a heart big enough for humankind (p. 16).

2. The class was told that this program of "The Ten Brave Christians" would especially welcome those who were discouraged and had nowhere else to turn, those who were afraid and had nowhere else to hide, those who were disappointed after having tried everything else, those who were lonely and wanted once again (or for the first time) to feel the great surge of God's love and power in their lives (p. 20).

3. You can't meet with people and pray with them and share your experiences without wanting to reach out and put your arms around them, because there is a bond of love that unites you. It changes your life (p. 22).

4. Things go differently when I start my day with God (p. 31).

5. God will come into your life through your Christian commitment— your total surrender to God (p. 32).

6. The purpose of life is not necessarily to be happy, but to have a life that matters . . . a life that matters begins with the total surrender of one's life to God . . . a life that matters REALLY MATTERS when we let God temper it through spiritual discipline (p. 33).

7. The Holy Spirit can work even when the preacher is on the "sidelines" (p. 36).

8. Total surrender to the will of God through Christ is essential to a Christian experience.

9. Until we surrender our lives to God and live in his will, no words can better describe us than, "We have played the fool" (p. 36)!

10. Can we help becoming discouraged when our religion becomes a load instead of a lift (p. 39)?

11. Christianity will propagate only when put into practice (p. 41).

12. To be a consenting child of God is to be surrendered to God through Christ, and committed to doing God's will (p. 45).

13. You should not be any more afraid to ask that God's will be done in your life than for your child to ask that your will be done in his or her life (p. 45).

14. Is the cross of Christ strong enough [to hold you]? Do you have faith in it? Look at the shame, the suffering, the sacrifice of the cross. Can you find anything in all the world that shows stronger love (p. 49)?

From How to Tell* a Church
(*as in recognize)

1. The authentic church may or may not be the one that is growing numerically. **But the real church, regardless of numbers, is the one**

whose mission is to be a servant. No church ever stands as tall as when it stoops to serve. The only solution is for the buildings to be the buildings and for the people to be the church (p. 4).

2. Because of my spiritual dryness, my next thought was: That is about all that can be said about my relationship to Jesus—that our feet were alike. I wanted to think that Jesus and I had more between us than feet, but at that time I couldn't. [From a sermon entitled: "Jesus Had Feet Like Mine"]

   Jesus had a healing touch, but I didn't! He brought forth the best in people, but I was down on everyone! He disciplined his time, but I was living carelessly! His prayer life was his strength, but mine was my weakness!

   I decided that on the following Sunday morning I would level with my congregation. I confessed that sometimes I felt that the only thing Jesus and I have in common is that we have feet that are alike. Together we began to look at Jesus' feet and our own. They had been victims of my dryness and now it seemed appropriate that I call to any of them who also felt dry and empty to come and stand with me. I invited all who could not say more of themselves than "Jesus had feet like mine" to come and stand with me. "If feet are all we have going for us in our personal relationship with Jesus Christ, I want us to discover how we can use them best" (pp. 24–25).

3. We can measure the church by how it looks at the humanity of Jesus. To take his humanity seriously does not raise questions about his divinity. On the contrary, it answers questions about his uniqueness. He was "very God *and* very man."

   Then it follows that the church is not ashamed of its own humanity. It affirms it. It recognizes that it is comprised of members and friends who are people with people tendencies. For us that turns out to be sinners. Its gospel is an invitation to repentance, an offer of forgiveness and a promise of personal redemption. **It will recognize sin as sin but will call the sinner *brother [sister]*** (p. 28).

4. The real church will pawn its steeple before it will neglect the needs of people (p. 29).

5. But there is absolutely no excuse for the church to procrastinate in specializing in spiritual vitality. Moreover, a church has forfeited its right to be if it fails to call people to respond to Jesus in the *now* (p. 42).

6. It is possible to take measure of a church by the number and depth of the new commitments that are being made (p. 42).

7. That church will also be planning creatively for even more significant spiritual encounters (p. 43).

8. If a church's mindset is to wait to function or serve until times and circumstances are favorable, the cross does not belong in it (p. 43).

9. That's what the church wants; that's what it needs. It has light and has had in every generation. But in a few generations it has also had fire (p. 57)!

10. Jesus is the "light that lighteth every man [woman] that cometh into the world." There is no question about it:
His church will teach his teachings.
His people will get equipped to minister in his name.
His light in his people's lives will overcome the darkness (p. 59).

11. We prefer the light—
when we insist on *knowing* and *having* the mind of Christ;
when we know the teachings of Jesus and discern how they can be applied to our circumstances;
when we are not only open to, but actively seek, divine guidance for our problems;
when we look for and find comfort and strength in relationships with other people who walk in the light (p. 60).

12. If the fruit of the Spirit is evident and the gifts of the Spirit are operative in the lives of the people, those people *act* like church (pp. 62–63).

13. When the Holy Spirit has truly come upon the church, the people will have an intuitive sense of knowing that their greatest treasure is not the power, or even the fruit, or the gifts of the Spirit. Their greatest treasure is *the Giver* (p. 63)!

14. The church cannot be all things to all people. But there is one thing it must be to all—a fellowship of caring people (p. 75).

15. . . . one of the missing ingredients in local church evangelism has been a concern for persons at the point of *their* needs and *their* interests (p. 76).

16. Consider a church that has a few hundred members today but can recall having twice that number. Yet milling masses pass its door every day. It has long been displeased with its plight. But not until it becomes fed up and disgusted with being a lame church will it have the desire to find creative ways to jump a rut and become redemptively involved with the people at its door (p. 79).

Next, do a thorough job of repenting. . . . A person can repent and a church can repent if the members have penitent hearts and genuinely want to care (pp. 79–80).

17. One other need is to consciously focus your concerns to care about specific persons who are all around you. Our tendency may be to be a friend of every man/woman which can be very impersonal. But we are called to relate meaningfully to specific persons who are close at hand (p. 80).

18. If the church does not influence people to make spiritual decisions, who will?

    The newspaper will!

    Television and radio will!

    The supermarket will!

    Playboy will!

    Politicians will!

    Business will!

    The chamber of commerce will!

    Listen, there are a thousand voices falling upon the ears of our people for every whisper the church can make (pp. 112–13)!

19. The pentimento process:

    There is a deeper dimension of the pentimento process. On extremely old and rare paintings, the oils become so transparent one can see the *original design* with which the artist started the painting.

    I discovered that the pentimento process can be applied to our lives. God created in me, and in you a unique masterpiece! But we can become overpainted, faded, and weatherbeaten.

    That speaks to me for I too must get in touch with the original design with which God created me or else live an aimless, fruitless, and unproductive life. . . . For our lives, the pentimento process will not be operative—we shall miss seeing God's original design—unless we have the input of spiritual vitality (pp. 114–15).

20. If the church is devoid of spiritual vitality at its own heart, it is less than the real church and will have no positive impact [for the community] (p. 115).

21. Coming to the end of your rope can be the best thing that ever happens to you. . . . When we are hurting enough inside we will be certain to cry out loudly enough to be heard and helped! "Into thy

hands I commend my spirit." That is still the best way to get off the
end of a rope (p. 129).

From Any Miracle God Wants to Give

1. It is better to pray the right way than the wrong way. It is better to
   pray the wrong way than not to pray at all. It is always right to pray,
   even if you do it the wrong way (p. 3).
2. A significant chunk of the joy of living is my growing understanding
   of what God and I have going with each other (p. 17).
3. "God, I know that the best thing that could happen to me is for Your
   will to be done" (p. 25)!
4. In my stumbling journey, I have found that I need deliberately to seek
   God's presence. The Great Experiment taught me that the more disciplined one is in prayer, the more conscious one is of God's presence in
   an ongoing way, and the less frantic he will be in crisis times. I have
   discovered a real connection between a conscious effort at
   communion with God and a sense of delight and joy in my life (p. 29).
5. More than my getting God to do something, prayer is my getting
   involved in what God is doing (p. 30).
6. I continue to pray knowing that God's love for me has absolutely
   nothing to do with "right" words, forms, rituals, or even whether I
   pray or not! I am learning that God's response to me will always and
   always and always be far greater than I can ask (p. 30)!

From Yearning to Know God's Will

1. I have concluded that discernment is a gift the Holy Spirit gives to
   persons seeking for special wisdom. All of us are called to cultivate,
   nurture, and increase our capacities to discern God's will (p. 9).
2. God wants *everyone* to know God's will. God doesn't withhold grace,
   play games, or tease us to test our faithfulness or our worthiness to be
   trusted with divine insight. I am convinced that God is far more prone
   to human revelation than I am to divine encounter. God's will is that
   you and I, everyone, and our faith communities should discern and act
   upon God's will (pp. 9–10).
3. The way of discernment is intended to be our higher way to be the
   church, but we often settle for a lower way—the adversarial approach

to make decisions by choosing up sides and taking a vote. We spend our time and energy arguing and defending various points of view, instead of using our energy to *listen* to know God's heart, God's mind, God's plan. The spiritual-discernment style of being together and making hard decisions is revolutionary, but it was practiced at "Ole' First Church, Jerusalem," and it is commended to our churches today (p. 14).

4. Discernment is about *seeing*. Silence is about *hearing* (p. 20).
5. Prayer and belief are inseparable. My 50–50 chance of needing surgery is an example. If I pray and "believe" in the negative 50, it will adversely affect my prayer and healing. Healing is enhanced as I pray and believe in the positive 50 (p. 25).
6. The promise of spiritual discernment is this: we can know and do God's will. God offers us an up-close and personal relationship. But we can never know God by studying God. We come to know God in the very process of our faithfulness to God—by doing God's will as we *know* it. The process stops if we are unfaithful to what we have *heard*, what we have *seen*, what we *know* to be God's will (p. 29).
7. . . . There are those happy occasions when either of two attractive alternatives could be lived out within the Spirit and love of God. At such times, it is as though God says, "Take your pick of either choice and go live your life!"
8. To think that God could put an idea into someone's mind and that person could comprehend that idea and immediately act upon it with unquestioning determination is the most remarkable wonder of all (p. 58)!
9. The major factor determining how little I communicate with God is the closed or underdeveloped ports of entry [emotion, imagination, memory, will, mind, body] to my consciousness (p. 76).

From Spirits Laughing

Our spirits are meant to laugh.
Humor is a spiritual gift.—p. 4

Humor is not something to be forced or whipped up or hurried. Humor is woven seamlessly into the fabric of our everyday, regular interactions, and that is the best way to focus on it and to work with it. Our personal stories and experiences of humor are there for us when we are ready for them. Natural humor (p. 11)!

Good humor is more than just humor that is funny. Good humor is fun to tell and is fun to hear. Good humor is helpful, uplifting, and therapeutic to the human spirit. Good humor has purity in its telling.

In today's humor market, there is an abundance of professional outlets for humor in the media, and there are about as many crass expressions of it. Humor that is vulgar, crude, demeaning, sick, cutting, vindictive, harsh, hurtful, sharp, ridiculing, or tawdry does the teller and the hearer a disservice.

Good humor gives hilarity the power to heal (p. 14)!

You are a humorous person! This bold assertion is undeniably true. You may not be successful as a **standup comic**. You may not tell jokes very well. You may not remember punch lines. You may not even be able to remember jokes. That's okay. Those abilities are based on learned, practiced, and cultivated techniques, and they are related to a very narrow range of humor that I refer to as **output humor**. Because the stand-up comic and the good teller of jokes frequently occupy center stage, the impression lingers that those are the only ways to be humorous (p. 15).

Good humor is like a cushion between people.
It is like lotion that keeps people from chafing.
It is a sweetener in any size pot (p. 39).

Think about these things:

1. The humorous person is not always loud and boisterous—and you do not have to be.
2. The humorous person is not necessarily the one who "keeps them laughing" all the time.
3. The humorous person does not *make* laughter but discovers reasons for laughter.
4. The humorous person cultivates an eye and an ear for humor and is sensitive enough to celebrate what others may miss.
5. The humorous person knows that humor and humorous happenings are special gifts that lighten the load and brighten the day (p. 54).

If you are in danger or anxiously waiting, you long for relief from the situation. You are eager to know when the danger has passed or the anxious waiting is over. Until that time comes, how wonderful and refreshing are those lighter moments of humor that punctuate the heaviness! How welcome is a genuine reason for laughter when the going is tough! We deeply value the ability to see, hear, or show the amusing side of things. Once we have experienced humor and a crisis together, we know they also belong together (p. 59).

Good humor and the desire and ability to use it are 100 percent good attitude.

A good attitude is intrinsic to good humor. Since it can be influenced or changed quickly, we need to check on our attitudes regularly. Doing an **attitude check** is the topic here: What is it? How do we do it? Why do we do it? When do we do it?

An attitude check is a check you make on yourself. Just be sure that you are checking upon your most significant attitude—the one you are conscious of right at this moment! At a later time you may wish to check other attitudes you hold—your attitude about global warming or paying taxes or of having to visit relatives this summer. These are attitudes worth checking on, but later.

Check on your attitude right now. Are you in over your head or feeling okay about things? Are you running emotionally hot about something, or do you feel cool and laid back? Right now, are you feeling positive or negative (pp. 73–74)?

Ask yourself, "How is my attitude right now—at this moment?"

If your attitude is good, do the following:

1. Consider why it is good and write some of the reasons.
2. While you have a good attitude, think of someone whose day you can brighten.
3. Write down their name and what you will do to brighten their day. Do it, while you feel like it!

If your attitude is bad, do this:

1. Consider why it is bad and write some of the reasons. Since your attitude is bad right now, go off by yourself until your attitude is good enough for you to be around other people.
2. While you are alone, decide what you will do about the reason for your poor attitude. Decide how much time you want to devote to wallowing in your poor attitude, and get ready to change it.
3. Think of yourself as a humorous person.

If you do "one" you will shorten the time for "two," and you will find yourself at "three"—on your way to a good attitude. Now you know how to do an attitude check. Check this every day. It takes sixty seconds (p. 85).

Some important principles about good humor

- You are, or can learn to be, a humorous person if you give attention to your outlook.
- Good humor has a healing quality.
- Since humor can be found in all life experiences if we look for it, we are our own best source of humor (p. 137).

Everyone needs, wants, and can benefit from a laugh. Remember that of all things you can give a person, a laugh is a treasure that is never used up. A laugh always comes with newness and has life of its own. Once the laugh has occurred, it can linger dormant for years and then come again with its original freshness. In a year's time, you can count on one hand when a laugh is not appropriate. It would take the stars to number the times a laugh is welcome.

Here you have been affirmed and encouraged in your use of good humor. You are not expected to make humor your full-time vocation, but why not consider making it your full-time avocation?

Look for funny things, memorize them, remember them, and tell them. You have the ability to do well in the school of humor. Be on the lookout for every good laugh because . . .

One laugh fits all!

The Living Prayer Center

The Upper Room Living Prayer Center was established in 1977 to fulfill the mission of Galatians 6:12: "Bear one another's burdens, and in this way you will fulfill the law of Christ."

This ministry is dedicated to raising prayer to a personal lifestyle. The Living Prayer Center is a unit of the Upper Room Program Area within the General Board of Discipleship. The financial support for the prayer ministry comes from Upper Room Ministries, the Commission of United Methodist Men, and individual gifts.

We help people seeking more specific direction and practical guidance in prayer and spiritual formation. We also assist those who want to be part of a prayer fellowship that is beyond the bounds of their local community.

The toll-free prayer line is a ministry of the Upper Room Living Prayer Center. The ministry is staffed by volunteers who receive calls in the safety and convenience of their homes, churches, or businesses. Training for participants can be conducted in the volunteer's area by a United Methodist Conference (District, Local) Prayer Advocate or by cassette. There is no cost for directing calls from Nashville to the volunteer's location. An information packet with full details is available.

The Upper Room Prayer Ministry offers an exciting international network of intercessory prayer and growth groups. These Covenant Prayer Groups respond to an average of ten thousand prayer requests a month. The Prayer Center coordinates the initial response to prayer requests; then they are sent for an additional thirty-day season of prayer to Covenant Prayer Groups. Each group agrees to meet at least once a month, though most groups meet twice a month or weekly. These groups are the primary setting for guiding supportive communities, spiritual growth, and outreach ministries.

Youth prayer groups will complete a preparatory study on prayer.

All Upper Room ministries are interdenominational, interracial, and international.

Contact The Living Prayer Center, P.O. Box 340004, Nashville, Tn., 37203.

Toll-free (for prayer requests) 1-877-899-2780–ext. 7214. www.jroy@upperroom.org.

The Academy for Spiritual Formation

I f you, like so many other Christians today, are experiencing a deep spiritual hunger, but have been unable to find ways to fill it, this information will be of interest to you.

The Academy for Spiritual formation is

- for lay and clergy persons who hunger for a deeper spiritual life. The Academy is open to all persons who are seeking God and wish to grow in Christian community with other seekers.
- a disciplined Christian community that emphasizes holistic spirituality, and nurtures body, mind, and spirit.
- a rhythm of study and prayer; rest and exercise; solitude and relationship.
- a rediscovering of our rich spiritual heritage through worship, learning, and common life.
- a time and space to discern direction, make covenants, and practice commitments.

Academy participants gather eight times during the two years. Each session is five full days, or forty days together. All participants are *in residence*; no commuters.

A typical day for each session includes Morning Prayer; Eucharist (combined with Evening Prayer); Silence; Covenant Group meetings; a morning and afternoon curriculum presentation, spiritual reading, and Night Prayer. Between sessions, participants covenant to deepen their spiritual life through journaling, spiritual direction, directed readings, and care of one's physical body. First year and second year covenant commitments provide a focus for one's spiritual growth.

Rationale

The Academy (a center for specialized learning and experience) recognizes that the Holy Spirit is the enabling power in Christian spiritual formation. It is designed to provide a setting for a spiritually disciplined community where lay and clergy can open their lives to receive God's love and grace to the end that they increasingly become spiritual leaven within the Body of Christ.

Audience

Lay and clergy who want to be a part of a community of seekers in order to learn the spiritual traditions of the church, to be open to God's spirit in new ways and to be further formed for Christian living and ministry.

Purpose

The purpose of the Academy is to provide an in-depth and comprehensive experience in spiritual formation for lay and clergy persons who are highly motivated in their sense of call to follow Christ and serve the church and the world. The sixteen courses offered over the two-year period, combined with the recovery of the use of Psalms in worship and the ongoing participation in personal and group spiritual guidance, are efforts to help prepare persons to live out that call.

For more information, contact the Academy for Spiritual Formation, (615-340-7233), or www.academy@bbs.upperroom.org.

About the Author

Nancy Pfaff received a bachelor's degree in education from the University of Nevada–Reno and her master's in Christian spirituality from Creighton University in Omaha, Nebraska. She is also a graduate of Diagnosis with Impact, a church consulting program at Fuller Theological Seminary in Pasadena, California, where she studied in the School of World Missions. Her training in leadership development took place at the International School of Theology in San Bernardino, California. In addition she completed the two-year Academy for Spiritual Formation.

Pfaff grew up in Minden, Nevada, a ranching community just fifty miles south of Reno. She taught business courses at the high school and university levels, and has worked for several non-profit organizations, including the Heart Association and the Ronald McDonald House. She also served as a missionary with Church Resource Ministries until she started her own church consulting business, Harvest Consulting Associates. Today the business name has been changed to Sacred Quest, which better describes her ministry of spiritual direction and retreats.

When not otherwise engaged, Nancy paints, writes, does handwork, and spins. Her pets include two frequently fertile zebra finches and a clown of a parakeet named Jo Jo. Her favorite hobby, however, is her young grandson, Taylor.